One Day at a Time

One Day at a Time

My Story of Lust, Loss, Hope, and Healing

Daniel J. Fick

WITH Allison Fick

WIPF & STOCK · Eugene, Oregon

ONE DAY AT A TIME
My Story of Lust, Loss, Hope, and Healing

Wipf & Stock
An Imprint of Wipf and Stock Publishers
199 W. 8th Ave., Suite 3
Eugene, OR 97401

www.wipfandstock.com

PAPERBACK ISBN: 978-1-5326-4885-4
HARDCOVER ISBN: 978-1-5326-4886-1
EBOOK ISBN: 978-1-5326-4887-8

Manufactured in the U.S.A.

To Isla Louise:

You are an exceptional child, and being your father is my joy. I want you to see the painting of my life colored by authenticity, faith, honesty, humility, love, repentance, and transparency. I hope this book, with all its destruction and hope, implications and importance, is part of the color palate.

I love you so much!

Contents

Acknowledgements

Recovery from addiction does not happen in isolation; we need both God and others. I am grateful for and indebted to many people who have supported me in my recovery. My friend, Paul, listened to and supported me during some of my life's most difficult moments. He may not remember our conversation outside a coffeehouse after my relapse in 2015, but I do. His friendship is invaluable (even though he supports Tottenham Hotspur). My sponsor, Craig, forced me to own my recovery. He is insightful, supportive, and authentic. I would not be where I am in my recovery journey without him. My therapist, Doug, is a brilliant psychologist. His expertise in human cognition and emotion has facilitated emotional, psychological, and spiritual healing once considered unattainable. He is the reason why I tell everyone to find a good therapist. My wife, Allison, is one of God's greatest gifts to me. This book would not exist without her support. She is a rare fit for my heart and demonstrates tangible grace to me every day (YAGTM). All of the above read drafts of this book, offering helpful insights. Of course, any remaining errors are my own.

Also, thanks to Wipf & Stock for accepting projects based on *merit* rather than *marketability*. I am grateful to partner together on another project.

Introduction

OUR LIVES ARE SHAPED by our experiences. My past shapes my present, which then affects my future. You are also being shaped. Your experiences have shaped you to potentially fit within one (or more) of the following groups: 1) Addict, 2) Victim, or 3) Cynic.

You may be an addict if you compulsively use lust (or some other behavior or substance) to cope with emotional issues. *Compulsive use* means continuing an attitude or action despite understanding its negative consequences. For me, compulsively using lust manifested in different ways, such as mental fantasy, masturbation, pornography use, or adultery. Now, *using* lust does not necessarily equate to *being* an addict. That is, not everyone who uses lust becomes addicted. However, if you find yourself compulsively using lust (or something else) to help you cope, you need to honestly assess your situation. Addicts may feel weary about *yet another* book about lust, pornography use, and adultery. You may be unconvinced that this book can offer help or new insight; you may be correct. Nevertheless, I hope you feel *less* isolated as you read this book. Isolation is so dangerous for those seeking recovery from addiction(s). Isolation provides opportunities to hide our addiction(s), which gives space for our addiction(s) to fester, creating a situation more dangerous than we may realize.

You are a victim if you have been the unfortunate recipient of *any* form of sexual misconduct. And victims are rightfully gaining a voice today amongst the #metoo and #churchtoo movements.

But as someone who lusts, and has both used pornography and committed adultery, I'm devastated that my attitudes and actions have contributed to the ever-growing list of victims. Victims may feel angry that *yet another* book about lust, pornography use, and adultery glorifies (by identifying) attitudes and actions similar to those that brought you pain. I hope this book shows you that real, active, and lasting recovery *is* possible, while, at the same time, validating your feelings of anger.

You may be a cynic if you believe you are immune to being caught in the snares of lust, consider my approach to recovery as either too conservative or too liberal, or doubt the reality of addiction or the harm in using pornography. Cynics may feel, well, cynical about *yet another* book about lust, pornography use, and adultery. However, great caution is advised if you find yourself believing, considering, or doubting any of the above. Various biblical texts warn against considering ourselves immune to sin — sexual or otherwise (1 Cor 10:12; Gal 6:1b; 1 John 1:8); both conservative and liberal approaches to recovery can be effective; science continues to aid our understanding of the brain and addiction; and many people have and will experience the harm associated with lust, pornography use, and adultery. If nothing else, I hope you begin to investigate *why* you feel cynical as you read this book.

Also, please note that certain parts of this book may feel tedious. This book isn't only autobiography; it also contains scientific, psychological, and theological insights relevant to my recovery journey. But don't avoid the tedious parts! Working through them may prove to be a balm to your weary soul.

And please don't expect a biblical exposition or theological treatise concerning the sinfulness of lust, pornography use, and adultery. Do I consider these attitudes and actions sinful? Of course. Am I going to say much more about their sinfulness? Probably not.

I've also been encouraged by my wife (who wants to protect my reputation) to mention two additional matters:

1. This book should be considered explicit. Of course, not every page is explicit; nevertheless, similar to the compact

discs I purchased as a teenager, this book should probably have a sticker affixed to the front cover that reads: "Parental Advisory: Explicit Content." The explicit parts are needed *so that* readers feel less isolated. That is, I'm not interested in shock value *per se*. However, writing in a manner that is too soft, vague, or opaque reduces "reader connectedness," and recovery is largely about *not* being isolated because you *feel* connected to something.

2. My current recovery is going well! I have been recovering from my obsession with lust, addiction to using pornography, and adultery for more than five years now, and am confident in my ongoing recovery journey. It hasn't been completely perfect (as you'll soon see), but I *am* recovering.

And another caveat: if you find yourself wanting to partake in similar attitudes and actions described in this book, you may *already* be ensnared by lust. I'm concerned that some may read this book, envy my past attitudes and actions, and feel enabled to lust, use pornography, or commit adultery. Of course, I can't control what you do; however, remember that each of us is responsible for *our own* attitudes and actions. I hereby absolve myself from "causing someone to stumble" because I'm not trying to convince you to operate outside your faith context (see Romans 14). *You* are responsible for *you*. Don't shift blame or responsibility.

Finally, I've decided to keep this book short on purpose. In fact, I've removed several chapters over the course of writing and editing. This decision was made because our ability to connect with each other via these pages is only so helpful. *Real* connection is done with *real* human beings, not pages from a book. Get out there and connect with others who share your struggle.

With all that said, let's begin . . .

1

Rock Bottom?

Word Vomit

"No, God; no!" Those words kept spewing from my mouth as I sped back to work. I had just committed physical adultery. You may be wondering why I specified *physical* adultery? Isn't adultery just adultery? Well, yeah; however, there seems to be differences between *physical* and *spiritual* adultery. For instance, *spiritual* adultery is far more pervasive. Of course, this doesn't mean that *physical* adultery isn't rampant; it is.[1] However, if Jesus's words are true that to even look at (i.e., desire or long for) a woman with lustful intent is adultery, then my *spiritual* adultery was (and probably still is) far more prevalent than my *physical* adultery.[2] Put differently, I could (and still do) commit regular *spiritual* adultery without committing actual *physical* adultery.

Now, before you get all super-spiritual, trash this book, and malign me on social media because I'm a nasty, perverted adulterer, perhaps pause for some personal reflection: First, are you *able* to be intellectually honest with yourself about your own struggle with spiritual adultery? And second, are you *willing*? If you are both able and willing, then it should be clear that we all succumb to regular,

---

1. Ashley Madison, the now-infamous "cheating site," has boasted more than "30 million people in more than 40 countries . . ." Lamont, "Life After the Ashley Madison Affair." To be fair, the legitimacy of the number of Ashley Madison users has been disputed.

2. Matt 5:28. See also Struthers, *Wired for Intimacy*, 58.

recurring spiritual adultery. If you are unable or unwilling, might you are afraid of admitting your own capacity for sin? Of course, acknowledging our adultery (whether spiritual or physical) should not be understood as overlooking, excusing, or accepting sin; rather, it should be seen as part of the process that stirs personal honesty, communal transparency, and repentance.

Acknowledging our adultery, though, often begets fear. Fear begs questions such as: What will my current wife think? What will my ex-wife think? What will my daughter think? What will my family of origin think? What will those who don't know this part of my story think? Is writing honestly and transparently worth the risk? Am I going to damage my future by writing this book? What if I experience a major relapse after this book is published?[3]

It can, though, also bring peace, which reminds me that:

> Because Jesus has already earned God's full approval and affection and acceptance for us, we no longer require any of that from anyone else. The gospel alone empowers and emboldens us to press on and strain forward with no anxiety over gaining other people's sanction or good opinion—even God's! All the care and love and value we most crave—full and final approval—we already have in Jesus.[4]

Fear and peace—both fighting for control.

Control

I don't like being a passenger in a car. Although I have to occasionally fill that role, I prefer to drive because I want control. Drivers, though, don't really have much control; it's just an illusion. The National Safety Council reported over 40,000 traffic fatalities in the United States in 2016.[5] If drivers really had control, these numbers should be much lower. In some peculiar way, though, these

---

3. Carnes, *Out of the Shadows*, 101.

4. Tchividjian, *Jesus + Nothing = Everything*, 92. True words from a fellow adulterer.

5. National Safety Council, "NSC Motor Vehicle Fatality Estimates."

statistics reduce my fear of writing this book because I've come to embrace two realities over the past few years: I am not in control of (1) lust's power, or (2) what others think of me.

I can picture some Christians raining down their condemnations as they read this: "You can't control the power of lust?! The Bible says no one born of God makes a practice of sinning!"[6] Fair enough. However, if *you* struggle to control your anger, pride, greed, envy, gluttony, gossip, etc., maybe we could be bunkmates in hell?[7] Banter aside; I should clarify the word "control."

Can you recall the Old Testament story of Samson and Delilah?[8] Samson, the last of Israel's judges, was blessed by God with unnatural strength. He needed nothing more than a donkey's jawbone to kill a thousand Philistine men.[9] The Philistines, enemies of Israel, were often on the receiving end of Samson's wrath. When the Philistine leaders learned that Samson loved a Philistine woman named Delilah, they used her to seduce Samson into revealing the secret to his unnatural strength. Seducing Samson isn't random; his struggle with lust has been documented.[10] However, this isn't the point of the analogy.

The point is to illustrate that Samson's strength was uncontrollable. After he lied to Delilah about the source of his strength, the Philistines attempted to restrain him. The result was not what the Philistines expected: "he snapped the bowstrings as easily as a piece of string snaps when it comes close to a flame," "he snapped the ropes off his arms as if they were threads," and "pulled up the pin and the loom, with the fabric."[11] Samson's physical strength is similar to lust's

6. 1 John 3:9. To be clear, though, John's point is that we ought to love one another (see vv. 10–12). Said in another way, Christians ought not practice not loving others.

7. For a comical yet convicting reminder of how we often overlook "permitted" sins, see Sprinkle, *People to Be Loved*, 121.

8. See Judg 16.

9. Judg 15:15.

10. Judg 16:1.

11. See Judg 16:9, 12, and 14, respectively.

strength, and the Philistine's pathetic attempts to control Samson is analogous to my pitiful attempts to control lust's power.

While in seminary, I looked for ways to practice the craft of preaching. One small local church provided several opportunities to hone my skills (i.e., embarrass myself). They were a kind, gracious, and generous group of people. I passed this church as I drove to commit adultery.

When I noticed the church, I remember thinking, "What are you doing?!" It felt like God was using memories of preaching at this church to convince me to stop what I was doing. Unfortunately, I kept driving. The power lust had over my life was uncontrollable. Although I had spent many Sundays preaching at this church about the redemptive work of Christ Jesus, my lust refused to concede.

Also, did you notice the second line of this chapter? I "sped back to work," which implies I left work to commit physical adultery. Of course, I didn't have to leave work to commit adultery; there were plenty of opportunities to "act out" by using pornography in a workplace bathroom. However, leaving work was another example of lust's incredible power over my life. I didn't ask to leave; I wasn't approved to leave; I just left. If I had been caught away from work without approved leave my employment could have been terminated, or, at minimum, I could have received some other type of workplace discipline. I was willing to risk losing my job to "act out." That's the power lust had over me.

Throughout my recovery journey, I've learned to surrender to the power of lust. Now, please don't misunderstand me; I'm not advocating surrendering *to* lust. Rather, surrendering to the power of lust means giving up the belief that *I* am more powerful than lust. Put differently, I've learned to surrender to the reality that if given an inch, lust will take a mile.

Also, "acting out" is a generic phrase I will refer to often that describes various addictive and compulsive behaviors. For me, I've "acted out" sexually by lusting, using pornography, masturbating, or committing adultery. But I've also "acted out" by binge eating to cope with some emotion, or unnecessarily washing my hands because I fear "contamination" (e.g., contracting some incurable disease from touching a door handle). I've also "acted out" by trying to please people.[12]

As I continue to recover from people-pleasing (as well as the other attitudes and actions listed above), I've learned that I can't control what other people think about me. Have you ever tried really hard to gain someone's approval, but every effort seems to fail? Despite your best efforts, this person does not approve of you, your attitudes, or your actions. This is an example of not being able to control what others think. Interestingly, life becomes much easier once we recognize our inability to control what others think.

Maybe you're reading this and appreciate my honesty and transparency. Or, perhaps you're reading this with contempt and disgust. Either way, those are *your* feelings. I cannot control them. You must identify and work through your feelings. In the past (and sometimes still), my oft-repeated attempt to gain a person's approval came from a so-called need to feel accepted. Being accepted by God wasn't enough (and, honestly, I didn't always believe God accepted me). Accepting myself as an image-bearer of God wasn't enough. I need(ed) *people* to accept me. I need(ed) validation. For me, lust, pornography use, and other women (than my former wife) were a means of meeting this so-called need.

False Validation

It's striking how much we seek validation. It's also striking how social media affects our feelings of validation. How many online friends do I have? Did my post get enough likes? Why can't I get more retweets?

Although I don't really use social media much, I used it in excess in the past. I could get lost on Facebook, spend hours looking at pictures on Instagram, and feel validated by my self-identified brilliant commentary on Twitter. More than once, though, I've

12. People-pleasing is a result of my codependency. To see if you may be codependent, go explore http://coda.org. Also, you can start codependency recovery by reading Beattie's *Codependent No More*.

realized that social media isn't healthy for my soul. I fell too often into the "social media black hole." I got drawn into too many pointless debates—the end result seeming to only be people becoming further entrenched in their position. And I also used social media to feed my lust.

It's ironic and embarrassing when I think about my hypocrisy. Many years ago I texted a fellow church volunteer to inform him that his tween son had posted pornography on a social media account. This is ironic and embarrassing hypocrisy because I had likely spent several hours using pornography the night before.

Now, I didn't wake up one morning, start cruising social media, and decide to commit adultery. My process was much slower. Nevertheless, social media had a direct role in my ongoing spiritual and eventual physical adultery. Over time, my brain needed more potency than the pictures and videos found on social media or pornographic sites. Those means were no longer sufficient to satisfy my lust (and, according to brain science, these images will *never* remain sufficient).[13] So what's more potent than pictures or videos of women I'll never meet? Actual women I could meet. And although I received a heavy dose of rejection from these women, searching for and contacting these women provided the new level of potency my brain craved for some time.

Social Media Mistress

It was only a matter of time before I met a woman online who didn't spurn my advances. I quickly moved our conversations from benign to sexual, using any form of available manipulation. And even though she laughed away my passive sexual propositions, she finally agreed to meet after I offered money in exchange for sexual favors. (So, in reality, I've solicited a sex worker. And, even though I wouldn't admit it then, I knew that's what I was doing.)

I left work as soon as she agreed to meet. Again, I didn't ask my boss if I could leave; I wasn't approved to leave; I didn't

13. See chapter 5, which discusses the harm lust and pornography use had on my brain.

make some excuse for leaving; I just left. No one needed to know. I could leave work, "act out," return to work, and continue with life unhindered.

After passing the church I'd preached at many times before, I pulled onto her street, scanning my surroundings as I looked for her house. Maybe I've seen too many episodes of *COPS*, but I couldn't ignore my fear of being arrested in an elaborate sex worker sting, which would ruin my ministry aspirations and, therefore, life. I'm embarrassed that my sole concern was protecting my ministry aspirations, with little concern for any other effects of physical adultery.[14]

Lifting the Veil

Have you ever driven by a run-down motel and thought, "The only things happening there are drugs and sex work"? Well, the motel we chose to "act out" at fit that mold. Thinking about it still makes me feel sleazy. As a self-appointed (and therapist-confirmed) germaphobe, entering a room like that should have been nearly impossible. And yet, there I was.[15]

Ironically, what had taken approximately two days to set up lasted maybe ten minutes. Now, I could provide more explicit details about our physical adultery; and, in some way, those details are important because they could help fellow strugglers connect to my story. And I want you to feel connected to my story because I don't want you to feel isolated. However, I'm going to spare you additional explicit sexual details because I think we can still connect on *how* my thinking was warped. My lust-obsessed thinking was so warped that I believed meeting this woman for certain sexual favors was *not* adulterous, as long as other specific sexually intimate acts were not performed. Can you see how crazy and warped my

---

14. "One of the greatest myths that allows the addict to repeat sexual behaviors is that it does not adversely affect other relationships, especially a marriage." Carnes, *Out of the Shadows*, 4.

15. Obsessive-compulsive disorder (OCD) can manifest as a fear of contamination.

thinking was? Eventually, a specific sexually intimate act was performed, which finally lifted the veil of lust from my eyes. And that was the moment: "Oh, God! What have I done?"

I couldn't go back. I was unable to return from not having committed physical adultery. I was filled with terror. I wanted to run away from everyone forever.

I learned later on in my recovery journey that one identifier of sexually compulsive behavior is the desire to separate oneself from the person, place, or thing involved in the act.[16] This was true of my situation, but I couldn't leave. I was unable to escape. I was not only her "john," but her courier. I tried to act calm and composed, like I had not just irrevocably changed my life, like my actions had not just greatly affected my reality. But I knew. I knew this rouse could no longer be maintained. And although I didn't yet know addiction/recovery language, I knew my life was "unmanageable." I knew my powerlessness over lust.

My Hope for This Book

Remembering your past, especially your sexual history, can be scary. Maybe it includes abuse or harassment. Perhaps you did stuff you wish you hadn't done. Or, like me, maybe you must admit some level of euphoria in recalling these events. We call this *euphoric recall* in the recovery community. It's real and scary. The real part is the ever-present reminder of the "brain high" experienced when "acting out." The scary part is the pain. Our past can be full of emotional, physical, and spiritual baggage that is burdensome and painful to carry.

So why write a book describing my failures? Why go through the embarrassment? Why open myself to contempt from other people, especially Christians?

I write this book, in part, because I hope sharing my story with honesty and transparency will be part of cultivating an environment that encourages others to be honest and transparent

---

16. Go to https://www.sa.org/test to test yourself about potential lust/sex addiction.

about their own struggles with addictive and compulsive behaviors (sexual or otherwise).[17] We all have "issues." Denying that reality seems strange. And yet a culture of fear, guilt, shame, and isolation exists, especially within the church. We don't want anyone to know about our "issues." We're afraid of being discovered. We don't want to be subjected to spiritual abuse. As such, I hope this book (1) helps some realize they aren't alone, (2) gives some the courage to acknowledge their "issues," and (3) relieves some of fear, guilt, and shame.

If you are currently within the recovery community, you can likely identify when you hit "rock bottom." This chapter depicts my "rock bottom." Actually, it depicts what I thought was my "rock bottom." My real "rock bottom" comes later. But before we get there, I want to discuss lust, addiction, and pornography use in my life.

17. See also Svendsen, *Fundementalist*, 10, 12.

2

Donuts

Lusting After Donuts

THERE ARE MANY GREAT resources on recovering from lust, addiction, and pornography.[1] Most, if not all, are more articulate and better researched than this book. Nevertheless, I'm offering my autobiographical perspective with the hope that if you don't read those books (although you should), then you'll get, at least, some information about these topics. In this chapter, I will explore lust, addiction, and pornography use in my life.

Lust is the unnatural filling of a natural desire. Therefore, lust is not *only* sexual.[2] For instance, I have a natural (i.e., biological) desire to eat food; however, this natural desire can be filled unnaturally if I eat only donuts. Donuts, albeit an excellent treat, do not carry the same nutritional qualities as other food items. An all-donut-diet is unsustainable. I would, though, live a donut-only lifestyle if I could. I want them all the time. And I sometimes use them to unnaturally fill my natural desire for real body-fueling food. This is my reality. I lust after donuts.[3]

---

1. See the Bibliography and Appendices for helpful resources!

2. To be fair, http://www.dictionary.com/browse/lust lists intense or illicit sexual desire as the two primary definitions. I, however, prefer the third definition: "a passionate or overmastering desire or craving."

3. Wilson, *Your Brain on Porn*, 64–65.

Lust Is . . .

I didn't really experience the cultural acumen of *The Simpsons* until adulthood. Some of my favorite episodes are from the "Treehouse of Horror" Halloween specials. In "Treehouse of Horror IV: The Devil and Homer Simpson," Homer sells his soul to the devil for a donut. Without spoiling the episode for you, Homer finds himself in hell's "Ironic Punishment Division," where a demon feeds him donut after donut after donut. The scene ends with an unfazed Homer finishing "all the donuts in the world."

For most of us (except Homer), we would eventually become full from too many donuts. Lust, though, is never full. Or, it can never be filled. Lust continues to crave. In today's culture, pornography can be a never-ending supply of "sexual donuts."[4] Some nights I spent hours upon hours scrolling, clicking, watching, fantasizing, always thinking the next pornographic image or video would finally satisfy my lust. And although the only act that *seemed* to satisfy was "acting out," in reality, "acting out" only restarted my addictive cycle (more on this later). This is lust. It is insatiable.

My favorite fiction novel is Tolkien's *The Lord of the Rings* (not very original, I know, but I'm invested enough to dedicate my lower right leg to Tolkien-inspired tattoos).[5] His imagination is remarkable; he literally created a language. And yet, his imagination is just that: imaginative. It's not real. The One Ring doesn't exist. Gandalf didn't actually fight Saruman. Frodo's finger wasn't really bitten off by Gollum. It's fiction.

I was around the age of 12 when I first masturbated. In bed one night, I simulated what I thought sex was like while fantasizing about a female neighbor. To simulate something is to feign, or, put differently, fictitiously represent something. Just like Tolkien's epic tale, fantasizing about my neighbor while simulating sex was also fiction. We weren't husband and wife. We didn't share a

---

4. Wilson, *Your Brain on Porn*, 142. See also Toates, *How Sexual Desire Works*, 335.

5. I must also note that my favorite historical novel is Michael Crichton's *The Great Train Robbery*.

meaningful relationship (she probably didn't even know I existed). She became a fictional character I used for sexual stimulation. This is lust. It is unreal.

An argument could be made that mewithoutYou is the greatest band of my generation. Their instrumentation, lyrics, and live shows are compelling. In 2009, they released a song called "The Fox, The Crow and The Cookie,"[6] which tells the story of a clever fox, a cocky crow, and a bumbling baker. In short, the baker shoos the fox away from his pastry cart, giving the crow an opportunity to steal some treats. Annoyed with the crow's opportunistic thievery, the fox uses cunning to persuade the crow into gloating about his accomplishment, causing the crow to open his beak and drop the treats to the waiting fox. Lust is similar to the fox in this song—it is incredibly cunning.

Lust used cunning to convince me that no one would be hurt by my actions:

- "No one will be hurt if I objectify a woman."
- "No one will be hurt if I use pornography."
- "No one will be hurt if I text random women."
- "No one will be hurt if I 'act out' with random women."

Do you see the progression? It starts small, but it doesn't stay small. I was convinced there would be no consequences, from both the seemingly insignificant use of pornography to the unmistakably adulterous rendezvous. This is lust. It is cunning.

As stated above, lust is the unnatural filling of a natural desire. It's insatiable, unreal, and cunning. It's also addictive. But what does it mean to claim sugar, TV, social media, lust, or pornography as addictive? Are we using this word in a legitimate way?

Perhaps we can answer this question by defining the word. *The Diagnostic and Statistical Manual of Mental Disorders* (hereafter, *DSM*) is used by psychologists and therapists to identify and

---

6. From the 2009 album *It's All Crazy! It's All False! It's All A Dream! It's Alright!*.

diagnose patient conditions.[7] The *DSM,* first published in 1952, has been updated about every 10 years; the most recent version, the *DSM-*5, was published in 2013.

I didn't find the word "addiction" when I checked the *DSM-*5; however, I did find the word "dependency."[8] The *DSM-*5 relates dependency to many different substances and processes.[9] Someone could be dependent on an external substance, like alcohol or drugs, or on an internal (or psychological) substance, like brain chemicals.

Have you ever watched a child taste sugar for the first time? My daughter's eyes lit up like headlights when she first ate sugar. Although she did not understand sugar's power *before* tasting her birthday cupcake, she wanted more *after* her experience. Something similar happens when we lust.

Our brains release a chemical called dopamine when we do things we enjoy. When we eat a birthday cupcake, go hiking, play the drums, read a good book, watch our favorite sports team beat a bitter rival, or participate in many other "healthy behaviors" our brains release dopamine. One problem, though, is that our brains also release dopamine when we lust (because, let's be honest, our brains enjoy lusting). Another problem is that we can become dependent upon the irregularly high and consistent level of dopamine our brains release when we lust specifically via pornography use. So, whether eating sugar, enjoying nature, watching Chelsea beat Tottenham, or lusting, you enjoy the sensations you're feeling, which leads to desiring more of this feeling, which leads to searching for ways to repeat the experience(s) that provided this feeling. This is lust. It is addictive.[10]

---

7. My therapist recently informed me that the *DSM* will eventually become obsolete as clinicians move away from the *DSM* towards the *International Statistical Classification of Diseases and Related Health Problems* (or *ICD-10*).

8. See also Struthers, *Wired for Intimacy,* 75.

9. American Psychiatric Association, *Diagnostic and Statistical Manual of Mental Disorders,* 350, 490, 541, 585.

10. Wilson, *Your Brain on Porn,* xii.

Not So Fast!

To be fair, the validity of process addictions (e.g., gambling, food, shopping, lust/sex, etc.) is contested. There are some who think "process addicts" (or "behavioral addicts") suffer from low impulse control, or are simply prone to compulsive behaviors. They consider the "science of addiction" too emergent for solid analysis. This all may be true; nevertheless, whether you call it "addiction," "low impulse control," or "being prone to compulsive behaviors," your life can be greatly affected by these attitudes and actions.

Interestingly, some sexologists believe pornography use is harmless, and even possibly beneficial. However, these scholars seem to only reference their own work, leaving out other corollary studies.[11] And the other side of the coin has some Christians treating addiction (to lust or any other addictive substance or process) as a simple sin issue to be resolved. "Just stop doing it," they'll say. But this response is unhelpful and non-pastoral for those of us struggling with addictive or compulsive behaviors. William Struthers, Associate Professor of Psychology at Wheaton College, rightly states:

> Using spiritual . . . language to describe the tenacious grip of sexually destructive patterns is helpful. But calls to pray harder, move the computer to the living room and get plugged into an accountability group only go so far. They come across as hollow to many men whose *brains have been altered and rewired* by their experiences with pornography.[12]

We can become addicted to both substances and processes (or behaviors) *because* we use them to cope with our emotions. Again, this doesn't mean lusting isn't sinful; it is. Nor does it mean we aren't responsible for our behavior; we are. However, we should also acknowledge that addiction and compulsive

11. See Wilson, *Your Brain on Porn*, 79, 155–57; also Struthers, *Wired for Intimacy*, 74.

12. Struthers, *Wired for Intimacy*, 15 (emphasis added).

behaviors are complex concepts. Part of their complexity is the cyclical nature of addiction.

The Addictive Cycle

In general, the addictive cycle looks like this:[13]

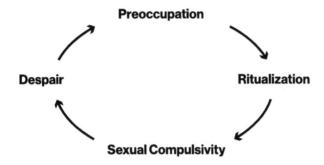

Let's now look at how each of these phases manifested in my life.

Have you ever watched the film *The Princess Bride*? Westley, a farmhand turned pirate, loves Buttercup, a farm girl turned princess. After three loveable villains (okay, two; nobody likes Vizzini) kidnap Buttercup, Westley's love compels him to climb the Cliffs of Insanity, recover from being "mostly dead," lay siege to a heavily guarded castle, and duel the loathsome Prince Humperdinck. All this for "true love." Despite being thought dead more than once, Westley continues to pursue Buttercup. He is engrossed with love for her.

The preoccupation phase in the addiction cycle is Westley and Buttercup's love story gone deviant. When preoccupied with lust, I would enter a trance-like state, completely captivated by thoughts of lust and sex.[14] Whereas Westley went on an obsessive search for Buttercup because of "true love," I found myself in an

---

13. Carnes, *Out of the Shadows*, 19–20. See also Wilson, *Your Brain on Porn*, 72–73; Struthers, *Wired for Intimacy*, 76–79.

14. Carnes, *Out of the Shadows*, 19. See also Struthers, *Wired for Intimacy*, 79–82.

obsessive search for sexual stimulation because of "true lust."[15] Although I could function in my daily life, my actions were similar to a horse with blinders.

Sadly, my obsessive search for sexual stimulation often resulted in objectifying women. It's disgusting that I objectify women. Whether sitting in a coffee shop, shopping for groceries, or walking a busy street, each occasion has been (and sometimes still is) an instance to pass females through my "sexually obsessive filter."[16] Instead of seeing women as God's wonderful creations, as someone's daughter, sister, wife, or mother, I often saw (and sometimes still see) women as an object for my sexual stimulation. It's shameful, I know. I hope God uses my shame to bring me and you to a place of honesty, transparency, and repentance.

The next phase in the addictive cycle is ritualization. This phase emphasizes special routines that lead to sexually compulsive behaviors.[17] Now, we all have routines. Most mornings you'll find me rolling out of bed, "micturating" (my brother-in-law's big word for peeing), and brushing my teeth. Some mornings may have alterations or variations; otherwise that's my routine. When struggling with addictive or compulsive behaviors, routines often intensify the preoccupation phase, adding significant arousal and excitement to a routine.[18] In fact, part of someone's ritualization phase could (perhaps unknowingly) include brushing their teeth.

For instance, if a husband uses pornography every morning after his wife leaves for work, and if he brushes his teeth prior to her departure, brushing his teeth could become an associated part of his ritualization process. This simple daily routine could add arousal and excitement to his morning because his brain associates brushing his teeth with using pornography. Now, brushing my

15. Carnes, *Out of the Shadows*, 19.

16. Carnes, *Out of the Shadows*, 20. See also Struthers, *Wired for Intimacy*, 45, 50.

17. Carnes, *Out of the Shadows*, 20.

18. Carnes, *Out of the Shadows*, 20.

teeth wasn't part of my ritualization process; however, getting into my car was one of my rituals.[19]

Each morning I opened my car door and became triggered to search for sexual stimulation. This often led to driving to and from work along routes I knew sex workers walked. Now, I didn't actually intend to "act out" with a sex worker. My irrational germophobia had me convinced that any form of contact with a sex worker, even non-sexual physical contact, would result in contracting some incurable STI (sexually transmitted infection).[20] However, making eye contact with sex workers was something I *could* experience without the fear of contracting an STI.

I often turned around multiple times, driving past them until they finally signaled for me to pull over. Once signaled, I knew this ritualized moment was over and I could begin searching for another sex worker to complete the next ritual. Each of these moments (and there were more than a few) began with opening my car door. As such, if trolling sex workers was part of my preoccupation phase, getting into my car facilitated (i.e., ritualized) my preoccupation by initiating arousal and excitement.[21]

In psychological language, *compulsivity* expresses a "strong, usually irresistible impulse to perform an act, especially one that is irrational or contrary to one's will."[22] I experienced an irresistible impulse to continue driving to my first adulterous rendezvous even while passing the little church where I had repeatedly preached (see chapter 1). My behavior was irrational and contrary to my will. Using women to satisfy my sexually compulsive desires is irrational. Bringing pain to the lives of others is contrary to my will. It's just not who I am, but it is what I did.

---

19. Carnes, *Out of the Shadows*, 51.

20. My therapist and I have concluded that I have a "fear of contamination." To help with my exposure therapy, make sure to shake my hand next time you see me!

21. Carnes, *Out of the Shadows*, 21.

22. See the third definition used at http://www.dictionary.com/browse/compulsion.

"Acting out," or compulsive sexual behavior, is the intended end result: the actual sex act.[23] I behaved in a sexually compulsive way when I committed physical adultery. But I've also acted in a sexually compulsive way every time I used pornography for sexual stimulation. Acting out, though, is not always an immediate action. I've spent long periods of time preoccupied with lust, completing various rituals before finally acting out several hours later.

Also, I'm not qualified to say whether someone could masturbate while using pornography and then consider that not a *compulsive* sexual behavior. William Struthers, a neuroscientist, seems to think that *use* does not necessarily constitute *abuse*, nor does *abuse* always equate to *dependency*.[24] For me, though, testing these boundaries is not a good idea. Could I handle driving really, really fast on the interstate? Probably. Is it a good idea to test that boundary? Probably not. Driving at or under the posted speed is much safer. So whether your desire is to honor God or simply not be an addict, steering clear (pun intended) of lust and pornography use seems best.[25]

My therapist once told me that when you start the ritualization phase, you may need more than 20 minutes of mental distraction for your brain chemicals to dissipate enough so that you don't complete the addiction cycle.[26] Addicts, like myself, need to avoid testing boundaries because we struggle to control, or stop, our compulsive behaviors without proper help.[27] Again, I often felt like a horse with blinders. The only thing I could see was the end result: acting out. I couldn't see anything else in my periphery. Acting out was the *only* possible result. And yet, I remember telling myself so many times to stop:

- "Dan, you're getting married; please stop."

23. Carnes, *Out of the Shadows*, 20.

24. Struthers, *Wired for Intimacy*, 75.

25. See chapter 5 for ways lust harms.

26. See Wilson, *Your Brain on Porn*, 126, 145.

27. Carnes, *Out of the Shadows*, 20. See also Struthers, *Wired for Intimacy*, 59.

- "Dan, you're a seminary student; please stop."
- "Dan, you're fathering a daughter; please stop."
- "Dan, you're becoming a pastor; please stop."
- "Dan, you've just committed physical adultery; please stop."

These are but a few examples of the seemingly countless times I've told myself to get my lust under control. And yet, without fail, I kept falling back into the same addictive patterns. Maybe I could "control" myself for a day, a week, even a month, but eventually I found myself returning to sexually compulsive behaviors. The result was despair. I felt powerless, hopeless, worthless, and afraid every time I returned to the same addictive patterns.[28] Every moment of despair solidified my belief that I was a failure.[29] I did not believe that freedom was possible. I did not believe I would ever be able to stop. However, I did believe I was disgusting, unlovable, and worthless.

On and On It Goes

I chose to display the addictive cycle as a circle because it is potentially endless. The addictive cycle often begins again as an attempt to cope with the intense pain and despair felt from acting out.[30] That is, I often tried to alleviate my despair by returning to sexual preoccupation because the dopamine release from my sexual preoccupation helped me cope with my pain and despair. Round and round it goes.

And so, the addictive cycle is like stoking a fire. If you keep stoking a fire, it should continue to burn. Of course, you also need to continue feeding the fire with tinder, kindling, and wood. So, if lust is a fire, and if the addictive cycle stokes the fire, then pornography was my main source of fuel. But what really is pornography?

28. Carnes, *Out of the Shadows*, 20.
29. Carnes, *Out of the Shadows*, 23.
30. Carnes, *Out of the Shadows*, 20.

Dangit, Mom!

My family vacationed a couple times in Southern California during my teenage years. On one occasion I found myself alone in our hotel room and decided to take a peek at the available adult video rentals. Naturally, my mother entered the room shortly thereafter. I quickly tried to change the channel, but she knew what I was doing.

Should the adult video rental advertisement be considered pornography? It likely contained titillating language and sultry images of women, but probably didn't display actual nudity. This question presents a particular difficulty when thinking and writing about pornography because different people have different answers when asked to define pornography. Your understanding of the nature of pornography is dependent on you and your experiences. So, for me, what is pornography?

Well, denying the pornographic nature of a hardcore sex website or softcore magazine seems strange. But what about your wife's lingerie catalog? The movie with the no-nudity sex scene? The television show without the sex scene but with random nudity? The adult video rental ad? Maybe considering how pornography has developed as a word will help.

Pornography Defined

Most contemporary English words have Germanic, Latin, and Greek roots. Pornography is part of this group. If traced back to its Greek roots, pornography derives from the word *porne*, which can be translated as "harlot for hire" or "prostitute."[31] This word functions like a noun, but there's also a verbal form, *porneia*, which is often translated as "fornication" or "whoredom."[32] So, we could

---

31. Kittel et al., *Theological Dictionary of the New Testament*, 580. See also Struthers, *Wired for Intimacy*, 27–29.

32. Kittel et al., *Theological Dictionary of the New Testament*, 581, 584.

define pornography as "fornication with a prostitute."[33] But does this ancient definition fit within our modern context?

If we follow the etymology of the word and can agree that pornographers are, in some sense, prostituting themselves, then this definition still seems to fit. Now, I'm not trying to shame or belittle those employed in the pornographic industry. As a pornography consumer, I'm not superior to the pornography creator. Moreover, we all have intrinsic worth just because we are human beings. Pornographers are, though, selling their bodies and sexual experiences to whomever will pay. So then, perhaps pornography (i.e., fornication with a prostitute) should be *anything* used as a means for extramarital sexual gratification? So, perhaps your *Men's Health* or *Cosmopolitan* magazine, your Netflix or HBO subscription, or any other "non-pornographic" website could actually be categorized as pornography? You may not be actually fornicating with a prostitute, but you have paid to act sexually towards them.

Regardless of the differences we may have about the nature of pornography, we should still affirm it as a destructive force, preaching the deadly lie that we are entitled to sex on demand.[34] This lie degrades both men and women alike. Both the creators and consumers of pornography can be objectified and dehumanized.[35] Pornography demonstrates to men that women are mere sexual objects for our penetrative pleasure, undeserving of value as equal partners.[36] Pornography demonstrates to women that men are selfish, don't care about intimacy, and can be violent.[37] And that's not where it ends.

Pornography also attacks our purity, which we should fight to protect, for the pure are blessed and will see God.[38] Purity, both in body and mind, is important for the Christian life. And sure, some have turned biblical purity into the awkward teenage-sexual-purity

33. Struthers, *Wired for Intimacy*, 19.
34. Struthers, *Wired for Intimacy*, 19.
35. Struthers, *Wired for Intimacy*, 19, 27.
36. Struthers, *Wired for Intimacy*, 58.
37. Struthers, *Wired for Intimacy*, 58.
38. Matt 5:8.

white-gown ceremony, but don't establish a false dichotomy as you try to avoid the aforementioned ridiculousness. I thought not having *direct* sexual contact with another woman would prevent me from committing adultery. But this mindset is just as ridiculous as the awkward white-gown ceremonies, because my mind had already committed adultery long before my body.[39]

From Then to Now

Explicit pornography has been available for thousands of years. Ancient Greece had pederastic paintings. The Kama Sutra was written and displayed as early as 400 BCE. Nevertheless, the explicit nature and present availability of pornography is unlike any other period of history, for we have the Internet, which permits both unprecedented explicitness and availability.[40]

The pervasive availability of pornography indicates its acceptance as a normal part of contemporary culture.[41] When I confessed my adultery and pornography use to some family members, one person expressed concern only with my adultery, and not my pornography use. This person seemed to not understand that my lust was so exacerbated by regular pornography use that I felt compelled to commit physical adultery.

Also, despite the normalization of pornography, people still seem to deny or minimize use. Unfortunately, the numbers indicate otherwise.[42] Of course, not everyone who denies or minimizes pornography use is lying, but many are. For Christians, denying or minimizing pornography use is not surprising. Most Christians feel great shame when they lust, use pornography, or commit other sexual sins. However, shame begets fear, which breeds silence and isolation. Whenever I gather with other groups of Christians, I often wonder how many people have

39. Struthers, *Wired for Intimacy*, 28.
40. Struthers, *Wired for Intimacy*, 19, 34.
41. Struthers, *Wired for Intimacy*, 21–22.
42. Struthers, *Wired for Intimacy*, 50–54.

recently used pornography, are addicted to lust, or feel like they can't share their struggles with anyone because their fear, guilt, and shame keeps them isolated.

If this is you, please know that my heart breaks for you. You don't have to be alone. You aren't alone. You don't have to suffer in silence. You can be free from fear, guilt, and shame. And I know you're out there. The numbers say so.

Numbers Don't Lie

An excellent resource on pornography use is the recent publication *The Porn Phenomenon*.[43] It's well researched, with accessible graphs, charts, and helpful analyses. The Barna Group, which conducted the majority of the research, offers results that are impossible to avoid and quite troubling:

- 49 percent of young adults believe their friends use pornography regularly.[44]

- 97 percent of people think pornography depicting children under the age of 12 is wrong.[45] (How is this not 100 percent?!)

- Adults 25 years of age and older think overeating (58 percent) is worse than viewing pornography (54 percent).[46]

- 14 percent of senior pastors and 21 percent of youth pastors say pornography use is a current struggle for them.[47]

Count the churches you pass the next time you drive around town. If you're able to count ten churches, the above statistics indicate that *at least* one senior pastor and more than two youth pastors employed at these churches *currently* struggle with using pornography. My guess is the numbers are higher than reported.

43. Barna Group and Josh McDowell Ministry, *Porn Phenomenon*.
44. Barna Group and Josh McDowell Ministry, *Porn Phenomenon*, 23.
45. Barna Group and Josh McDowell Ministry, *Porn Phenomenon*, 61, 71.
46. Barna Group and Josh McDowell Ministry, *Porn Phenomenon*, 65.
47. Barna Group and Josh McDowell Ministry, *Porn Phenomenon*, 158–59.

Despite the reported anonymity of the surveys and claimed candidness of its participants, the numbers are probably not an accurate representation.[48] As a former pastor, I can attest to staying silent and isolated because of my fear, guilt, and shame. To be forthcoming about my addiction to lust and pornography use (even to an anonymous source) could lead to the destruction of my ministry aspirations. However, my isolation also allowed me to quietly spend lots of money on pornography.

In 2009, William Struthers estimated the United States spent 12 billion dollars on the sex industry. This amount is just over 20 percent of the estimated financial size of the worldwide sex industry (57 billion dollars).[49] For some perspective, Namibia's gross domestic product is lower than what Americans spent on the sex industry in 2017. In fact, the American sex industry had greater market value than Swaziland, Burundi, and Liberia combined.[50] This means if Americans stopped paying for sex, we could literally fund three African countries. If the sex industry's profit margins are correct, then sex sells. And if you're consuming pornography (whether buying or just using), then you're contributing to its demand. This is often a tough pill to swallow for those of us who also believe pornography use is detrimental to society.[51]

One More Thing

Oh, and one more thing before we continue. Lust is also harmful. In chapter 5, I'll identify how lust harmed my brain, heart, and relationships.[52] For now, though, I want to discuss the development of my faulty core beliefs, wherein I cultivated an unhealthy belief system that facilitated my addiction to lust and pornography use.

48. Barna Group and Josh McDowell Ministry, *Porn Phenomenon*, 134.

49. Struthers, *Wired for Intimacy*, 20.

50. "List of Countries by Projected GDP."

51. Struthers, *Your Brain on Porn*, 23.

52. Visit https://fightthenewdrug.org and https://www.yourbrainonporn.com for helpful articles on how pornography harms our brains, hearts, and relationships.

3

Core Beliefs

Old Saint Nick

MY NINE-YEAR-OLD DAUGHTER STILL believes in Santa Clause. She doesn't have a reason to not believe. The influencing forces around her have not yet confirmed otherwise, and these forces weigh heavily on this magical, and mostly harmless, belief. What is not surprising is that her belief in Santa Claus has also affected her belief in other magical beings, like leprechauns, fairies, mermaids, and the Easter Bunny. The day she discovers these magical beings don't exist will be a sad day. Her sensitive heart will likely break as she loses part of her innocent childhood.

As we develop into adulthood, we build different belief structures. And what we believe—both positive and negative—is often a reflection of the influencing forces around us.[1] Not just about magical beings like Santa Claus, but other important beliefs about culture, politics, religion, etc. In fact, we also create beliefs about ourselves, which can be called "core beliefs."[2]

---

1. Wilson, *Your Brain on Porn*, 70.
2. Carnes, *Out of the Shadows*, 15.

Choice Filters

Core beliefs are, often if not always, the filters through which we make choices.[3] However, these beliefs can become faulty if negatively disrupted. Patrick Carnes, a leading expert in addictive and compulsive behaviors, has identified four core beliefs developed during childhood that play a critical, and often problematic, role in the life of a potential addict:[4]

1. Self-image: how children perceive themselves
2. Relationships: how children perceive their relationships with others
3. Needs: how children perceive their own needs
4. Sexuality: how children perceive their own sexual feelings and needs

Although faulty core beliefs are common amongst those struggling with addictive and compulsive behaviors, each person appropriates these beliefs in different ways because we all have a unique story. As such, I want to personalize and summarize *my* faulty core beliefs:[5]

1. I perceived myself as a bad person, unworthy of unconditional love and acceptance.
2. I perceived my relationship with others as conditional because they would surely abandon me once they discovered the "real me" (i.e., the lust-obsessed, pornography-using, eventually adulterous me).
3. Only I can meet my needs *because* I am unworthy of unconditional love and acceptance and will be abandoned once people discover the "real me."
4. My greatest need is sex. A life without sex is not worth living. I must indulge my sexual impulses as they arise, whenever they arise.

3. Carnes, *Out of the Shadows* , 16.
4. Carnes, *Out of the Shadows* , 97.
5. Carnes, *Out of the Shadows*, 16.

Now, my faulty core beliefs should not be confused as being good or healthy. Certainly not! Nevertheless, they *are* my core beliefs, and I am actively working towards rectifying them.

Conditioned Love

A necessary condition states that without x you can't have y. For instance, to win the league you need a keeper that stops shots. Or, without a keeper that stops shots (x) you can't win the league (y). Now, that's not the only thing needed to win the league (you also need players to score goals), but you can't win the league without a keeper that stops shots.

Unfortunately, human beings often have necessary conditions for love. That is, our offer of love is, often if not always, contingent upon x (and, sometimes, a, b, and c too). Maybe not always or with everyone, but human beings seem unable to truly love without conditions. This is a bitter pill to swallow, but true nevertheless. But does this mean God loves conditionally too? Is God's love for and acceptance of me conditioned upon x?

Now, cognitively speaking, I don't actually believe God loves conditionally. However, for reasons I've not yet traced to their genesis, I have struggled (and sometimes still struggle) to emotionally accept God's unconditional love for and acceptance of me. Perhaps this is due to the negative view of self that American Christianity has ingrained within me.

Although not always overtly stated, American Christianity seems to teach that humans are bad, unworthy people.[6] That's what the Bible says, right?[7] But in relation to what, or whom, are we supposedly bad and unworthy? Doesn't the Bible also say humans are created in God's image?[8]

Now, I'm not denying the overall human problem of sin, so relax. However, I am questioning what it means to be a sinner

6. Carnes, *Out of the Shadows*, 99.
7. Ps 14:1–4; Eccl 7:20; Rom 3:9–18, 23; Eph 2:1; 1 John 1:8.
8. Gen 1:26–27; 5:1; 9:6; 1 Cor 11:7; Jas 3:9.

and whether being a sinner equates to automatically labeling ourselves as bad, unworthy people. To whom are we unworthy? Why are we bad?

Human beings are sinners *because* we have attitudes and actions that are sinful. However, these attitudes and actions are sinful *because* they are contrasted against an infinitely holy and righteous God, not other people. So although I may be actually "bad" in comparison to God, people (you and me) often believe our role is to playact as God and confer badness or unworthiness upon others.

If nothing else, this paradoxical dichotomy—wretched sinner *and* image bearer—is rather perplexing, especially for a young person. So, embracing a healthy understanding of self has been difficult for me, and I have instead adopted the faulty core belief that I'm a bad, unworthy person—unworthy of God's love, unworthy of human love, and unworthy of self-love. And so, as my lust became more difficult to control, I became determined to keep my compulsive sexual behaviors hidden. I didn't want to offer any additional ammunition for conditioned love from God, others, or myself.[9]

The "Friend Zone"

I was the perpetual "third wheel" (also, "fifth wheel," "seventh wheel," etc.) during my teenage years. Most friends "dated" in high school, but I did not. I was chubby, grungy, and *always* in the "friend zone." I was often identified by female peers as "marriage material," but never considered present-day "dating material." Experiencing this constant rejection, sharply contrasted with the romantic acceptance enjoyed by many other friends, resulted in feeling unlovable.

Feeling rejected and unlovable was also exacerbated by my belief that I would be abandoned if people discovered the "real me" (i.e., the lust-obsessed, pornography using me).[10] What would my

9. Carnes, *Out of the Shadows*, 108.
10. Carnes, *Out of the Shadows*, 109.

female peers think if they knew I lusted after them? Would they no longer want to be my friend? Could anyone be romantically involved with me if they knew I struggled with lust?

Long after my teenage years, this faulty core belief was reinforced when my fomer wife indicated her desire to separate. Now, I don't fault her for this. Although maybe not the best option, her separation and eventual divorce from me were biblically valid.[11] My regular pornography use and adultery turned her into an actual trauma victim. Her mind and heart need to be treated with the same care as other types of trauma victims. Nevertheless, her request to separate and eventual departure reinforced both my first faulty core belief that I am a bad person, unworthy of unconditional love and acceptance, and my second faulty core belief that I will be abandoned by anyone who discovers the "real me." Can anyone love me as I am?[12]

Everyone's Inadequate

The third faulty core belief is about how children perceive their own needs. For me, I was unlovable and unworthy. As such, no person or thing could meet my needs, except for me. The "real me" will only be abandoned, so depending on others to meet my needs will only result in failure.[13]

God is inadequate. He's constantly angry and disappointed with me. His conditional love shrivels with every sin I commit.

Family is inadequate. They don't even know the "real me." And if I admit my obsession with lust and pornography use, any chance I had to receive love and acceptance from them would be ruined.

Friends are inadequate. Even though my closest friends are like family, we stopped having *real* conversations about sexuality

11. Can we please stop insisting that God "hates" divorce? A better translation of Mal 2:16 is "the man who hates [or does not love] and divorces his wife . . ."

12. Carnes, *Out of the Shadows*, 101, 109.

13. Carnes, *Out of the Shadows*, 102, 110.

long ago. Or, if we did discuss this issue, we didn't really move beyond surface-level sterility. Emotional, mental, and spiritual health became individual matters, and were not engaged within a healthy community.

So, the only available option seemed to be figuring out *how* to cope with lust and pornography use on my own. This was not a good idea. My brain was already convinced that I *must* feed lust. But remember, lust is insatiable. It cannot be satisfied. My never-ending search to satiate lust only resulted in more lust. My attempt to control lust demonstrated my lack of control. Unfortunately, one result of my never-ending, never-satiated quest to quench my lust was the ingraining of the fourth and final faulty core belief—sex is my most important need. And lust and pornography use never failed to solidify this pseudo-need.

Flip That Switch

Unless you're living under a rock, you can't deny the sexualization of our culture. Actually, the "pornification" of our culture is probably more accurate. We seem convinced that the act of sex is always long, steamy, vocal, and mutually orgasmic. Oh, and everyone engaged in the act of sex is always impossibly attractive. In fact, our breath never smells bad. Our crotch never smells like "crotch." Even "quickies" are mutually orgasmic. Of course, anyone who's had sex (and is honest) realizes that sex is quite odd, although this reality remains largely unspoken.

Converse to Hollywood's depiction, sex requires vulnerability. It sometimes results in frustration, loneliness, or fear. It can be short, utilitarian, quiet, and only orgasmic for the guy. However, sex can also be a beautiful expression of deep intimacy with another person.

When the time is right, I hope to talk with my daughter about human sexuality from both a biblical *and* scientific framework. Saving sex for marriage and then maintaining a monogamous sexual relationship with her spouse is a biblical prescription *because* God wants what's best for his creation. Put differently,

God's moral commands are not abstract rules for her to follow just because he's a jerk. How so?

When we orgasm, our brains release a chemical called oxytocin. Oxytocin is a "binding" chemical, meant to bind you to your mate.[14] God's directive to avoid fornication and adultery is, in part, because he wants us to be bound to one person, not many.[15]

However, American Christianity proclaims a confusing message about human sexuality. Before marriage, sex is not only off limits but also sinful. Various "scare tactics" (e.g., teenage pregnancy, sexually transmitted infections, abandonment, shame, etc.) are used to get young people to avoid being sexual. Of course, after proclaiming your wedding vows at the marriage altar, sex must immediately morph into this wonderful, guilt-free, sinless blessing from above. Although many Christian young people (especially Westerners) hear nothing more than "don't have premarital sex" for the first few decades of their lives, they are expected to immediately flip the switch to the blessed experience of simple, never-difficult, always-guilt-free sex. And despite how it may sound, I'm an advocate for post-nuptial, monogamous sexuality. But can we really expect Christian young people to not be confused about human sexuality?

So what was I to do? I was an unmarried Christian teenager with intense sexual desires. I feared I might never marry because I had not yet experienced any type of romantic reciprocity from female peers. And my lust was convincing me further that the "real me" (the lust-obsessed, pornography-using me) was unworthy and unlovable because of my intense sexual desires. I believed sex was my greatest need, and I felt trapped, scared, and alone. There's no way I could talk to anyone about this.

14. Struthers, *Wired for Intimacy*, 105.

15. The use of "sexual immorality" in 1 Thess 4:3 is a translation of the Greek word *porneia*, which can be understood as generalized sexual vices, including fornication and adultery.

Error Message

This has been a difficult chapter to write. Seeing how your past shapes your present experiences is tough. Nevertheless, I must work through and share my internal pain and struggles because I also desire emotional, mental, and spiritual health.

If nothing else, I want my daughter to see me admitting error *because* I am not perfect, make many mistakes, and desire her love, acceptance, and, when necessary, forgiveness. If I practice the humility of admitting error, hopefully she will feel comfortable talking to me about anything—especially her missteps.

I also want to encourage everyone reading this book to begin investigating and acknowledging their own faulty core beliefs. And if you're a family member of someone struggling with addictive or compulsive behaviors (lust or otherwise), please be open to also identifying and understanding your faulty core beliefs, pain, and contribution to any broken family situation(s).[16]

Faulty core beliefs are dangerous because they coax us into unhealthy attitudes and actions. Although lust eventually convinced me that sex was my greatest need, I didn't become addicted to lust and pornography upon first glance. However, impaired thinking, as a result of faulty core beliefs, gave lust and pornography use the foothold needed to become the means for unhealthy addictive and compulsive sexual behaviors.

16. Carnes, *Out of the Shadows*, 95–97.

4

Meeting Porn

Where Were You?

DO YOU REMEMBER THE first time you saw pornography? Was it at a friend's house? At night on your computer? On your iPhone in bed? An adult magazine you found stashed somewhere?

The following is my attempt at an honest and transparent appraisal of the major developmental moments of my obsession with lust and pornography use. Sharing these embarrassing and painful details is important because I want you to feel connected to my story. Although I've left out certain explicit details to avoid potential triggers, I hope you still connect with my story enough to understand that you're not alone in your struggle with lust or other compulsive sexual behaviors.

First Glance

Compared to the extreme pornography available today, my introduction to pornography was relatively tame—a ripped-out page from some unspecified pornographic magazine hidden under the carpet of my friend's bedroom closet. But there she was—a beautiful blonde woman exposing herself.

What a rush of emotions! I felt exhilarated looking at this naked woman, intrigued about exploring her body, and yet uneasy.

As a young teenager, I was unsure how to act around my friend in this arousing (and quite awkward) state.

Muscle Magazines and Fuzzy Channels

To the best of my knowledge, my father did not use pornography when I was a child, so pornographic magazines were not stashed around our home. And I was a teenager long before the advent of high-speed Internet, so endless opportunities for free pornography was not yet available. However, I wanted *more* after seeing this beautiful, blonde, naked woman. So my search began.

(As an aside, please don't assume your tween or teenage child is *not* using pornography. If you are making this assumption, please stop being naïve. Recent research indicates that 20 percent of teenagers use pornography every week.[1] Start having *real* conversations with your children. Share *your* pain and struggles. Don't *only* speak *against* harmful attitudes and actions. Don't *immediately* punish harmful attitudes and actions. Seek first to understand *before* being understood.)

Until my sophomore year in high school, my only options were different types of "non-pornographic" media.[2] I would use department store catalogs, with attractive, full-busted women modeling underwear, or lingerie catalogs sometimes found as I stuffed newspapers into mailboxes along my paper route. If I had a couple dollars to spare, I would buy a muscle magazine's "bikini issue," because their female models came as close as possible to "pornographic" nudity.

I wasn't yet old enough to purchase actual "pornography," so these bikini issues became my most used form of "non-pornographic" pornography. When I found lingerie catalogs in someone's mailbox (which was rare), I was always too nervous to take them home to use for acting out. And I only used department store catalogs

1. Barna Group and Josh McDowell Ministry, *Porn Phenomenon*, 149.

2. My definition of "pornography" in chapter 2 would actually identify these types of "non-pornographic" media as pornography.

when nothing else was available; they just weren't as sexually enticing as the lingerie catalogs or bikini issues.

When I purchased a muscle magazine's bikini issue, my first task was to tear out pictures of the most attractive female models. Once this task was completed, I could maintain my secret obsession by hiding these prized pictures and disposing of the remaining magazine. The best way to remain undiscovered was to put the remaining magazine into our kitchen trash, remove the trash bag, and place it into our outdoor trash receptacle. In hindsight, I've wondered if taking the trash outside looked suspicious, because what teenager volunteers to do household chores?

Hiding these pictures was a bit more difficult. I couldn't use my bedroom to hide these pictures; that was too risky. There were too many unforeseen circumstances that could lead to someone discovering these hidden pictures. Our basement, though, seemed like an ideal hiding spot. Within our basement was a storage room, and within that storage room was a closet. Near the ceiling of that closet were heating and cooling vents. My *modus operandi* was to fold these pictures in half and place them on top of the vents in the basement storage room closet.

However, my ingenious hiding spot was not without problems. The kids' bathroom on the second floor offered the most privacy for acting out because it had a door lock. But every time I wanted to use these pictures to act out, I had to smuggle them from our basement to our second-story bathroom and then back to our basement. For some time, smuggling these pictures was worth the risk. Eventually, though, something happened that forced me to reconsider this method of satisfying my lust.

After using these pictures one afternoon to act out, I moved with cautious haste from behind the locked bathroom door. I quickly crept down the first flight of stairs, my contraband neatly folded under my shirt. To my dismay, though, I encountered my father standing in the kitchen. He lifted his head as I hurried past, and inquired about my fast descent into the basement. With pangs of fear, I insisted he "hold on," also mentioning that I'd "be right back." Now, I don't remember what happened after returning from the basement.

That is, I don't remember being asked any further questions about my strange behavior. Nevertheless, the "walls of discovery" felt like they were closing around me. There must be an easier way to satisfy my obsession with lust. Enter "fuzzy channels."

These channels quickly became my new go-to form of pornography. Once my family was asleep, I'd sneak down the hall past my sisters' and parents' bedrooms, descend our staircase (avoiding the steps I knew creaked), turn on the television (hoping someone had not left the volume blaring), and stare. My retinas burned as I looked unblinking at the television. But not blinking seemed worthwhile, as my determination was often "rewarded" with seconds-long moments of clear nudity and human sexuality.

As I consider past behaviors, my use of both "non-pornographic" muscle magazine bikini issues and pornographic "fuzzy channels" were likely fueled more by curiosity and intrigue of the unknown, rather than the powerlessness and unmanageability manifested in later years.

Identifying what fueled my behavior is important because, similar to William Struthers, I'm not convinced *every* teenager lusting and using pornography is destined to be an addict.[3] They may just be curious, exploring their budding sexuality. Nevertheless, their emotions and actions could lead to impaired thinking and, potentially, future compulsive sexual behavior(s) if not addressed with wisdom, love, and care.

STBs

Most friends I had as a teenager were holdovers from childhood. We'd grown up together, most of us attending the same church and private school (located on the same campus). School days, Wednesday night church, Sunday morning (and often evening) church, and lots of other extracurricular school and church events were spent together.

---

3. Struthers, *Wired for Intimacy*, 75.

Much of our time together consisted of pulling pranks. We pulled traditional pranks like toilet-papering homes or plastic-wrapping cars of friends and rivals, but we also enjoyed more unusual pranks. Many weekend nights were spent filling paper lunch bags with poop and burning them on the porches of random people. However, unlike Billy Madison, who had enough self-respect to use dog poop, we used our own poop (yes, you read that correctly).

Although I'm not sure whether my parents even know about my poop-burning pranks, our other ridiculous, albeit innocuous, pranks had my mother correctly referring to me and my friends as STBs (Stupid Teenage Boys). Generally, teenagers act "stupid" because they face conflicts and disparities that breed confusion. For instance, my friends and I lived in the tension between accepting and rejecting lust and pornography use. On the one hand, most of us, if not all, were obsessed with lust and using pornography, and therefore "accepted" lust. On the other hand, we all would have affirmed that lust and pornography use were to be avoided because of our Christian roots.

My Very Own Porn Dealer

During high school, a friend from church and school became my very own "porn dealer." Interestingly (and probably unfortunately), my "dealer" was the older brother of the friend that had first shown me the pornography hidden under his bedroom closet carpet. As a sophomore in high school, I was unable to purchase and, to the best of my knowledge, had not yet possessed an actual "pornographic" magazine. My dealer, a senior in high school, was both able to purchase and willing to provide me with regular pornographic magazines.

For the next several months, he provided magazines when able. These magazines introduced me to new levels of explicitness. Never before had I seen close-up female anatomy and graphic sexual poses.

I did not usually keep these magazines long after receiving them from my "dealer." My punishment would have been far greater if caught with these magazines than if caught with muscle magazine pictures. So I still had to resort to the aforementioned muscle magazines and "fuzzy channels" when I wanted to act out but didn't have access to the now-discarded pornographic magazines.

Adults Only

The attitudes and actions of my younger years planted the seeds of addiction. However, my addiction didn't take root and grow until adulthood. And even then, its new growth was slow. As a poor college student living with his parents, I could rarely afford to purchase pornography. Over time, though, lust convinced me to spend the little money I had, promising both sexual satisfaction and protection from being discovered. I often found myself at the local corner store, awkwardly requesting a magazine from behind the counter, trying to convince the attendant I was buying it "for a friend."

Over time, my use broadened. Many lonely Sunday afternoons were spent renting pornographic movies from the "adult" section of the neighborhood video rental store or purchasing them from "adult" novelty stores. Although my fear of discovery was waning, it wasn't non-existent. I would always move with speed and care, ever afraid of being caught with pornography at the rental counter or seen leaving the novelty store. There had to be a more private, discreet way to feed my obsession with lust. And there was. Its name: Internet pornography.

Becoming Enslaved

Becoming enslaved to Internet pornography wasn't immediate; it was a gradual process. My obsession with lust and pornography use waxed and waned during my college years. When it waned, I clung to the belief that the supposedly unlimited amount of sex

38

that came with marriage would finally satisfy my obsession with lust and pornography use. (Of course, the idea that being married equates to an unlimited amount of sex is false—just ask any married person! And even if I could have unlimited sex, this would not likely curtail my obsession with lust.) When it waxed, lust and pornography use took me to new and, sometimes, extreme forms of pornography. Nothing illegal (because I know you were wondering); however, I've probably used every other type of pornography you now imagine as "extreme."

What's eerie, although not surprising, was the similar progression taken by both my former and latter pornography use. My former pornography use was still print images, whereas my latter pornography use was also still images, but *online*. The Internet provided quick and easy access to both "non-pornographic," yet alluring, images of my favorite female celebrities as well as explicit pornographic images. However, even these unlimited online images eventually lost their potency. My brain soon required greater stimulation. I needed something similar to the pornographic movies I had been renting or purchasing. I was thrilled, then, to find many free clips of pornographic movies on the Internet. Like I said, both followed a similar progression.

These free pornographic movie clips introduced me to a new form of pornography: "reality" porn." Over the next dozen years, "reality" pornography was my favorite form of pornography to use. Despite many attempts to stop using, "reality" pornography continued drawing me back. It seduced me, convincing me that the events portrayed in these "real" videos could also happen to me.[4] My friend's sexy mom or hot sister would eventually try to seduce me, an attractive woman would swap sexual favors for a ride into town, or my sultry teacher would trade good grades for sex. Of course, the events portrayed in these videos are *not* real. Other people we encounter throughout the day are *not* interested in exchanging sex for goods and services (except for, maybe, sex workers). Unfortunately, one result of lust changing my reality included becoming more brazen with using pornography. My lust

4. Struthers, *Wired for Intimacy*, 35.

continued lusting for more lust, so I began using pornography outside the safety and privacy of home.

Work and School

I worked as a janitor (or custodian) during high school and college. Some of the bathrooms we serviced, especially within industrial settings, had pornographic magazines stacked on the toilet tanks. I became quite proficient at simultaneously scrubbing toilets and glancing through these magazines. After I graduated from college, I took a year-long hiatus before entering graduate school (i.e., seminary). During this hiatus, I worked as a delivery driver for a small floral warehouse. I spent my days delivering boxes of flowers to different local flower shops. Sometimes when I returned from an evening delivery to an empty warehouse, I would grab a pornographic magazine from our front office and act out in the bathroom.

In these moments, the fear of "missing out" was how my powerlessness over lust manifested. If I didn't look at these pornographic magazines, I might miss out on seeing the *most* beautiful naked woman *ever*. And if I missed out on seeing the most beautiful naked woman, I would be depriving myself. Why would I want to deprive myself? Why would I want to risk missing out on finding the woman that would finally (supposedly) satisfy my lust?

After being admitted to seminary, I began looking for another job with better pay and greater flexibility. I was interested in teaching, so I began working as a substitute teacher in a local school district. After a year of substituting, I secured a temporary position as an in-school-suspension facilitator. I arrived at work each morning and enjoyed several hours of quiet, uninterrupted time before the suspended students arrived. (I basically got paid to review Greek flashcards and read assigned theological texts.) Unfortunately, I also began using this quiet, uninterrupted time to feed my obsession with lust. My classroom was separated from other classrooms, which meant I could spend hours fantasizing, using pornography, and acting out behind my locked door. Now, I wasn't brazen enough to use pornography on the school district's computers, but I often brought my personal laptop to use pornography when mental fantasy just wasn't enough.

Interestingly, though, I was brazen enough to use my seminary library's computers to use pornography. Most of the library computers were positioned to avoid private viewing; however, some were positioned in such a way that minimized the threat of discovery. One particular computer was my favorite.

This computer faced away from all other computers. The only real threat of discovery was someone sneaking up behind me, which was difficult in our older, creaky-floored library. Wanting to further minimize my threat of discovery, I often opened several legitimate webpages or computer programs, moved the pornography I was using to one of the lower corners of the monitor, and then, if approached, would quickly click on something legitimate to cover the pornography. I would often watch pornographic videos for hours, all under the guise of studying the Bible and theology.

Whacking It on My Wedding Day

I became gainfully employed and married my fomer wife midway through seminary. Gainful employment meant disposable income, which led to new horizons in lust and pornography use. I shudder when thinking about the thousands of dollars spent feeding my obsession with lust. One new horizon was phone sex. As a teenager, I'd call toll-free numbers and drool over the sexy-voiced advertisements. I longed for the day I could discover what was beyond the recording that begged me to input my credit card number. I could now fulfill this fantasy.

I had just finished applying a coat of paint to the walls of the apartment I was soon to share with my fomer wife and decided to "reward" myself with some phone sex. I felt powerful choosing which woman would fulfill my every sexual request. I was consumed with lust as she described her physical appearance. I sat in the doorway of my new bedroom, acting out to my false reality, fully content with feeling accepted by this random woman.

A couple weeks later, I also decided to act out on the morning of my wedding day. I was convinced this was acceptable behavior. My rationalization was that I wanted to actually enjoy my wedding day, and not be solely focused on the forthcoming wedding night. And I didn't use "pornography" *per se* to act out, but a sex scene from a "non-pornographic" movie. "If the movie doesn't have explicit nudity, then it's not that bad, right? And even if it is, I will soon leave this life of lust behind because of all the rapturous, guilt-free sex I will have soon," I thought.

But sex wasn't easy for us. Now, I'm *not* blaming our difficult sex life for *my* moral failures. Trying to and having sex with my former wife was sufficient for our "honeymoon phase." Unfortunately, these marital privileges soon became insufficient, and I began to feed my obsession with lust once again. I don't remember the exact timeline, but pornographic videos (even "reality" porn) eventually became insufficient, and I began looking elsewhere to satisfy my lust.

Onward and . . . Downward

Although I had phone sex a few more times, I never felt completely satisfied afterwards. Did the woman on the other end really look as sexy as she sounded? I wanted to both hear *and* see the women I encountered. So I began using video chat rooms, which allowed me to both hear *and* see the women. "Perhaps now I have found the outlet that will help me feel connected! Video chat rooms will finally and ultimately satisfy my lust!"[5] Or so I thought.

But I really believed that because it was reinforced by several women who convinced me that our "connection" was deep and lasting. Of course, our "connection" was about them getting paid. They didn't *really* care about me. They weren't *really* interested in establishing a deep and lasting connection. They just wanted to get paid. And yet, I was content to dump dollar after dollar into their accounts so I could continue interacting with them, always

---

5. Struthers, *Wired for Intimacy*, 66–67.

hoping they *really* cared about me. I just wanted to feel desired. Accepted. Loved.

As you can probably predict, video chatting with these women eventually wasn't enough.[6] The "connection" began to dwindle. I needed something more tangible. So I sometimes offered money to exchange phone numbers with them. And then I offered even more money to meet up with them. If we could just call or text each other, then I'd be satisfied. If we could just have sex, then I'd be satisfied, right?

After being rejected many times by women from these video chat sites, I decided to turn my attention towards "real" women — those living within my general location. I've never been audacious enough to have an affair with anyone I know, but I did once meet a woman on a much-used video chat site who also lived in my home state. Although she denied my requests to exchange phone numbers and meet, the new thrill, my new high, was pursuing "real" human interaction. At this point, I rarely used pornography for acting out. And I soon found someone on social media who wanted to "connect" with me. The unmanageability of my obsession was coming to a head. My life was unraveling. Lust was destroying my brain, heart, and relationships.

6. Struthers, *Wired for Intimacy*, 67.

5

That's Bad for You!

A Formal Argument

ONE ROLE I HAVE is teaching philosophy to college students. Philosophy has four main divisions: axiology, epistemology, metaphysics, and logic. Logic is the study of correct reasoning (or thinking). If we understand how to correctly reason, we should be able to form good arguments. However, we need to understand what an argument is *before* we can form good arguments. And, despite popular opinion, an argument is *not* merely a heated exchange of words. It does not have to be a verbal battle with raised, angry voices. Instead, an argument can be a calm, rational exchange of ideas, because it's really nothing more than a group of statements.

Now, that last clause is a bit hyperbolic, and my description of an argument needs further unpacking. This group of statements that creates an argument includes at least one premise and a conclusion. A premise sets forth the evidence, or reasons, to believe the conclusion, which should be supported by the premise(s).

I would like to offer the following argument for *why* we ought to avoid lust:

P1: Lust harms our brain.

P2: Lust harms our heart.

P3: Lust harms our relationships.

C: Therefore, lust should be avoided.

So far, this argument is "strong," which means the conclusion follows probably from premises we *assume* are true. A better argument, though, is "cogent," which means it has premises that are *actually* true. This chapter seeks to demonstrate that the aforementioned premises are, in fact, true.

Cocaine Brain

Unless you're addicted to cocaine (and maybe even if you are), you will likely agree that cocaine is bad for you. And yet, people still use cocaine. According to the 2016 National Survey on Drug Use and Health, nearly 39 million Americans used cocaine that year. That's more than 10 percent of living Americans! What's worse is that cocaine use grew between 2015 and 2016.[1] How can this be? If cocaine is bad for you, why do an increasing number of people use this drug?

People use cocaine because specific chemicals that make us feel good are released when part of our brain's reward center, the ventral striatum, becomes activated.[2] And this activation and subsequent chemical release inclines us to return to whatever substance or behavior brought about this release. Interestingly, sexual stimulation and cocaine use activate the same part of the brain (methamphetamine and heroin use too). To be fair, this research was not completed on humans, but rats. Nevertheless, these findings have caused some addiction specialists to affirm the similarity between process (or behavioral) addictions (e.g., lusting, eating, gambling, shopping, etc.) and substance addictions (e.g., nicotine, alcohol, cocaine, heroin, etc.).[3] Now, I've never used cocaine, but I've never needed to because I've had ample opportunities to "get high" on lust.

1. Substance Abuse and Mental Health Services Administration (SAMSA), *Results from the 2016 National Survey on Drug Use and Health: Detailed Tables*, 235–40.

2. Wilson, *Your Brain on Porn*, xiii–xiv.

3. Wilson, *Your Brain on Porn*, 72, 75, 78–79; Struthers, *Wired for Intimacy*, 97.

An Unstable Hostage

Our brains, the complex and magnificent creations that they are, have several regions with various roles in releasing different chemicals that make us feel good. These various "pleasure centers" are the means by which people "get high" on both substances *and* behaviors. And just like Pavlov's dog, our brains learn to respond to certain stimuli and conditions.

Unfortunately, our brains aren't as intelligent as we'd like (despite their complexity and magnificence). They are prone to exploitation, and can be hijacked without realizing what's happening. Like a hostage who's oblivious to being captured, the brain is not astute enough to recognize that lust is its captor.[4]

A hostage in a suspense movie should be considered unstable if they accept their captor's behavior as "good." And yet, this is what our brains do. Our brains don't recognize lust's hijacking as problematic *because* they are created to accept and enjoy the released chemicals and, furthermore, desire their continued release.[5]

Johnny and Sally Caveman

There once was a man named Johnny Caveman. One day, he went hunting for dinner. He came upon a large buffalo, which he killed and ate for dinner. Having consumed this fatty, calorie-dense, protein-packed meal, Johnny Caveman felt satisfied, resolving to hunt for more buffalo the next day.

Johnny Caveman's resolution to hunt again was a reaction to a chemical called dopamine. Dopamine affects our desire to seek.[6] It motivates us to pursue, provokes initiation, tells our brain to "get," and preps us for its next release.[7] Because of dopamine,

4. Wilson, *Your Brain on Porn*, 86.

5. Wilson, *Your Brain on Porn*, 86.

6. Weinschenk, "100 Things You Should Know about People." See also Wilson, *Your Brain on Porn*, 65.

7. Wilson, *Your Brain on Porn*, 58–59, 65. See also Struthers, *Wired for Intimacy*, 90, 101.

Johnny Caveman remembered the importance of hunting as a means for satiating his hunger. His reaction to dopamine was a survival mechanism.

Hunting for food, though, was not the only ancient survival mechanism. Propagating the human species was also understood as such.[8] In order to maintain a clean gene pool, our ancestors need-ed to avoid inbreeding. So, Johnny Caveman set out to find Sally Caveman, a novel—and quite necessary—sexual partner.[9] In fact, Johnny's search for novelty released dopamine, which encouraged Johnny to keep searching for more novel sexual partners.[10]

Let's be careful, though, to recognize a major difference between Johnny Caveman's search for novelty and our own. For Johnny Caveman, a novel sexual partner, like Sally Caveman, was necessary to avoid making babies with parents or siblings *because* there were so few people. We do not share this same problem today. Our world boasts more than seven billion inhab-itants; certainly enough for every person to have one mate and still avoid inbreeding.

The explosion of the Internet has had both a positive and negative impact on our innate search for a novel mate. Although many have found loving, meaningful, and lasting relationships on-line, many others have become enslaved to constantly browsing the seemingly endless online supply of novel sexual partners.[11] Maybe it's not lust or pornography that people are actually addicted to, but rather novelty.[12]

Now, whereas dopamine incites Johnny and Sally Caveman to "get," DeltaFosB, a protein unit of pleasurable memory, urges them to "get while the getting is good."[13] In fact, dopamine preps individuals for its next release by facilitating the accumulation of

8. Struthers, *Wired for Intimacy*, 92, 97, 101.

9. Wilson, *Your Brain on Porn*, 58. See also Carnes, *Out of the Shadows*, 87.

10. Wilson, *Your Brain on Porn*, 14, 60–61.

11. Wilson, *Your Brain on Porn*, 60–61, 84.

12. Wilson, *Your Brain on Porn*, 139.

13. Wilson, *Your Brain on Porn*, 85.

DeltaFosB. You could think of dopamine as the boss, instructing DeltaFosB to accumulate.[14]

One running joke within my family revolves around family projects. My mother seems to always take the role of manager, while her children are her laborers. She once sought my help hanging several family pictures high above a staircase. From the safety of the ground, she directed my father, younger sister, and me as we traversed the wobbly scaffolding. Now, I would never expect my mother (who's had both knees replaced) to navigate high scaffolding. My point is to use humor to illustrate the relationship between dopamine (my mother) and DeltaFosB (my father, younger sister, and me).

Trailblazing

Now imagine you're hiking through the woods, blazing a trail where one does not yet exist. You happen upon a picturesque place, a view so breathtaking you resolve to soon return. Thankfully, the pathway you created is now both embedded and accessible. Moreover, each time you return, you further fortify the pathway, making it even more accessible. Maybe one day you'll even decide to pave the trail, continuing its fortification and accessibility.

With every release, dopamine facilitates either creating or reinforcing "brain pathways."[15] Given enough time and effort, a once crude path could become a nicely paved neuro-highway. The creation of neural pathways, including the potential transition into neuro-highways, is because our brains are "plastic."

Plastic Brains

In 1907, a Belgian-American chemist named Leo Hendrick Baekeland invented Bakelite. For most of us, both the inventor and

---

14. Wilson, *Your Brain on Porn*, 85.
15. Struthers, *Wired for Intimacy*, 100.

invention are likely unknown. And yet most of us, if not all, have used something today that is a result of his invention: plastic.

Plastic—bendable, flexible, and prone to influence—is used today in many ways. Consider all the plastic things you use throughout your day. Leo truly revolutionized our world.

Our brains are also "plastic." They are bendable, flexible, and prone to influence. Now, our brains aren't plastic the same way Tupperware is plastic. I'm not going to use a brain to store my Chinese leftovers. Rather, our brains have what scientists call *neuroplasticity.*

Neuroplasticity refers to the changes our brains undergo as a result of our experiences. Every thought you have creates, reinforces, or changes your neural pathways. And the connection becomes stronger as you continue thinking about something or return to a behavior because neurons, or brain cells, that fire together, wire together.[16] Our neurons send (i.e., fire) electrical signals that strengthen their connection (i.e., wire), and the more they fire together, the stronger they wire together. I both created and reinforced an unhealthy neural pathway as I increased my pornography use. This pathway became deeply embedded, making it difficult to escape this well-worn path, which resulted in *desensitization* and *tolerance.*

Don't Tolerate Tolerance

Desensitization and *tolerance* are partners in the addictive process, and unlikely to be foreign concepts because of widespread alcoholism and drug abuse. Many people have been affected by these tragedies, or, at minimum, understand their devastating effects. If you regularly consume large amounts of alcohol, you will eventually become *desensitized* to, for instance, drinking a single beer. That is, your body will be able to *tolerate* more alcohol, so you will have to

16. Wilson, *Your Brain on Porn*, 68.

consume larger quantities to achieve the desired effect.[17] This is essentially how desensitization and tolerance work together.[18]

The results of desensitization and tolerance also hold true for those who lust and use pornography.[19] As I spent hours preoccupied with lust, my brain released an excessive amount of dopamine.[20] The more dopamine my brain released, the more tolerant I became. The more tolerant I became, the more dopamine I needed to experience the desired effect.[21] Ironically, our brains start to reduce the released amount of dopamine to protect us from excessive (i.e., chronic) stimulation.[22] Unfortunately, smaller quantities of released dopamine only caused me to lust more so that I could continue to experience the same high.

As my neurons continued firing and wiring together, I needed more potency to satisfy my dopamine cravings. I used explicit forms of pornography and even began searching for tangible ways to interact with other women to increase my dopamine release. Similar to a drug addict craving a purer substance because it will provide a better high, I craved something with greater potency to satisfy my lust. Although my pornography use began with a ripped-out page from a pornographic magazine, I eventually committed physical adultery because my brain craved so much dopamine. Of course, that's not the only reason for my physical adultery, but it is the biological reason.

17. In general, this is also true for other drugs like cocaine, heroin, and methamphetamines.

18. Wilson, *Your Brain on Porn*, 66.

19. Wilson, *Your Brain on Porn*, 79.

20. Wilson, *Your Brain on Porn*, 65.

21. Wilson, *Your Brain on Porn*, 37–38, 80; Struthers, *Wired for Intimacy*, 76.

22. Wilson, *Your Brain on Porn*, 66.

THAT'S BAD FOR YOU!

Recapping Premise 1

Premise 1 states that lust harms our brains. I hope to have shown how this first premise is *actually* true. So let's recap what we've learned.

First, when sexually stimulated, our brains release a chemical called dopamine and accumulate pleasure-memory protein called DeltaFosB. However, both the release of these chemicals and our response(s) to them are not inherently harmful because these chemicals are also released and responded to when we complete healthy behaviors (see chapter 2).

Second, our brains have neuroplasticity and create different neural pathways. Neuroplasticity and the creation of neural pathways also does not seem necessarily harmful because our plastic brains can also be shaped by healthy behaviors.[23] So, then, why is lusting and using pornography harmful to our brains?

Although we can shape our brains in healthy ways, we can also shape our brains to respond to unhealthy stimuli, like lust and pornography. And our brains aren't smart enough to recognize that lust has taken them hostage. As we lust or use pornography, we become desensitized and tolerant, requiring greater amounts of dopamine to experience the same results. And again, the problem is not with the release of dopamine and accumulation of DeltaFosB. Rather, the problem is that our brains are not meant to be constantly deluged with excessive amounts of dopamine.

With this evidence before us, we should affirm that lusting, using pornography, and using cocaine all have the same effect on our brains. Put differently, substance addictions are essentially the same brain disorder as process (i.e., behavioral) addictions.[24] Of course, acknowledging a disordered brain does *not* necessarily excuse behavior. But excuses are different than reasons. Excuses attempt to deflect blame. Reasons seek to explain. I'm *not* trying to excuse my (or your) compulsive sexual behavior. Nevertheless, lust and pornography use did change my brain. Lust and pornog-

23. Wilson, *Your Brain on Porn*, 36.
24. Wilson, *Your Brain on Porn*, 75.

raphy use promised acceptance and relief from sexual tension, but instead left me with a terrible addiction to a false reality.[25]

Kardia

The second premise indicates that lust harms our hearts. Now, I don't mean our biological hearts. Lust doesn't cause cardiovascular disease (at least not that I know of!). Rather, lust harms our spiritual elements. The Bible often denotes the "heart" as the innermost part(s) of the person.[26] It is the dwelling place of our emotions, intellect, and will.[27]

My heart has been greatly affected by lust's lies. But don't be fooled; I participated in planting lust's lies. You may have also participated in planting your own lies. Interestingly, proficient lying is often a necessity for addicts. In order to continue feeding our obsession, addiction, or compulsive behavior, addicts must often juggle multiple lies (and sometimes even multiple lives).

But as great a liar as I've been, lust is far better. Lust's cunning ability to manipulate my faulty belief system facilitated my acceptance of the destructive lies mentioned below. And these lies damaged my spiritual elements. These lies were planted in the fertile field of my impaired thinking, which harvested an unmanageable life.[28]

Not Enough

The first, and perhaps most devastating, lie I believe(d) is that God is not enough for me. This isn't a new lie; people have believed it for millennia. God was not enough for Adam and Eve, which is why

25. Doidge, *Brain That Changes Itself*, 107. See also Struthers, *Wired for Intimacy*, 13.

26. See John 16:22 (ESV), Rom 10:6, and Eph 6:22 (ESV).

27. Kittel et al., *Theological Dictionary of the New Testament*, 612.

28. Carnes, *Out of the Shadows*, 23–25. See also Struthers, *Wired for Intimacy*, 37.

they took and ate the forbidden fruit.[29] God was not enough for David, which is why he raped Bathsheba and murdered Uriah.[30] God was not enough for Ananias and Sapphira, which is why they were dishonest to Peter about withholding some of the proceeds from a property sale.[31]

The causal link between the choices of those mentioned above seems to be idolatry. Essentially, idolatry is placing something before God.[32] I commit idolatry every time I try to satisfy myself with something other than God *because* I don't believe he is enough for me.

Now this doesn't mean I can't find satisfaction in a good cup of coffee, or Chelsea beating Tottenham, or a sexual experience with my wife. It does mean, however, that pizza may be an idol if it ultimately satisfies me more than God. I idolize more than I realize.

I often find myself trying to fill my "God void" with things only God can satisfy. This conceptual phrase ("God void") has become painfully cliché, however C. S. Lewis seems correct when he states, "If I find in myself a desire which no experience in this world can satisfy, the most probable explanation is that I was made for another world."[33]

Part of my recovery journey has included recognizing my spiritual problem. And part of my spiritual problem is believing that God is not enough for me so I must fill this void with something else. Lust often volunteers to be this filler. But lust never ultimately satisfies because I'm made for another world. I'm meant to be satisfied by something (really, someone) else. In fact, the truth is God *is* enough for me. David believed he lacked nothing *because* God was his shepherd.[34] This can be true for me (and you) too!

---

29. Gen 2:16–17; 3:1–6
30. 2 Sam 11:4, 14–17.
31. Acts 5:1–11.
32. Exod 20:3; Deut 4:15–19; 5:7.
33. Lewis, *Mere Christianity*, 136–37.
34. Pss 23:1; 34:9–10.

Of course, accepting this truth is not easy. I can believe this lie at times. I still struggle to live within the truth that God *is* enough for me.

And there's no magic formula for achieving intimacy with God. Well, maybe the formula is Christ Jesus, but every person must still connect the dots between believing a proposition (e.g., God loves me) as true and *actually* experiencing this belief. Thankfully, I also believe that God is gracious and patient, and recovery is about progress, not perfection.

Conditional Love

A second lie I believe(d) is that God's love is conditional. Conditional love is based on *doing*, rather than *being*. It's about *action*, rather than *identity*. Certain conditions must be met to receive "love" (or "acceptance," "approval," etc.).

Unconditional love, however, is based on who you *are*, rather than what you *do*. I hope to mimic the unconditional love offered by Christ Jesus. I hope my daughter knows that my desire is to love her unconditionally, regardless of what she *does* (good, bad, or otherwise). She has my love and acceptance because of who she *is*, not what she *does*. But unconditional love is not always easy to extend.

During the early stages of my recovery journey, a pastor and now former mentor implied that his support (i.e., acceptance or approval) of my recovery process would be based on submitting to his plan of action. Submitting to his plan of action allowed him to control my recovery, for my failure seemed to also be his failure. His plan of action instructed me to limit attending individual therapy and recovery group meetings for "more church fellowship." But "more church fellowship," at least in this situation, would have resulted in being bludgeoned with hollow theological platitudes, rather than developing a safe environment where real authenticity could take place. These people did not, or perhaps could not, understand. This is but one example that shaped and reinforced my belief that God's love for and acceptance of me is also conditional.

Now, I'm not against church fellowship. And I may be wrong that "more church fellowship" would have been unhelpful for my situation. Maybe "more church fellowship" *is* the cure for what ails me? Nevertheless, my concern with the idea of "more church fellowship" is that I've spent the majority of my life believing this would fix my obsession with lust and pornography use, but to no avail. Again, William Struthers seems correct when he states that "calls to pray harder, move the computer to the living room and get plugged into an accountability group only go so far."[35] Perhaps churches pushing an agenda that equates lasting recovery (for whatever ails you) with only "more church fellowship" or "better theology" is not the most helpful idea?

Although this pastor and now former mentor's approval and acceptance were conditional, God's is not. God loves, approves, and accepts me (and you!) *without* condition. God's love is secure and steady, free to love and accept me for who I *am*, rather than what I *do*. In fact, God loves and accepts me despite my actions.[36]

I've Earned This!

"I studied all night and still failed my school exam!"

"I worked really hard on this work project and still got passed over for the bonus!"

"I pursued my spouse all day and still was denied sex!"

Have you ever uttered one of these statements? If you have, you may remember how frustrated you felt with the end result. Despite maximum effort, your grade was lower, your bank account hadn't increased, and you weren't having sex as much as you "deserve."

When we feel like we "deserve" something, we can create what is best called a "sense of entitlement." As a white American male, I'm familiar with feeling a sense of entitlement. I often believe I'm entitled to *x*, when, in reality, I've done *nothing* to earn

35. Struthers, *Wired for Intimacy*, 15.

36. Rom 5:8; see also Luke 15.

x. Now, maybe we did work hard for a better grade, deserve the financial bonus, or feel like we'd earned sex. However, great caution is advised here because entitlement is such an alluring lie. Entitlement screams:

- "I'm really stressed out! I'm entitled to masturbate while using pornography."
- "I haven't used pornography since last week! I've earned lusting after him/her."
- "If she doesn't want to have sex with me, then I deserve to have sex with someone else!"

There were countless times I believed this lie. However, I'm *never* entitled to lust (and neither are you). Despite my stress level, how long I've abstained from using pornography, or how often my wife rejects me sexually, I don't deserve to lust. I haven't earned it. I'm not entitled to it. If I was, Jesus would not have equated lust with adultery.[37]

Just a Little Bit

My wife and I have been eating a ketogenic diet for a while now and the results have been great. The purpose of this diet, which people follow for a variety of health outcomes, is to put your body into ketosis. Your body reaches ketosis when carbohydrates and sugars are limited or eliminated. If carbohydrates and sugars are not avoided, you may disrupt ketosis and impair whatever health goals you are working towards. This diet seems all-or-nothing.

However, a ketogenic diet does allow for some flexibility. While vacationing in Michigan a couple summers ago, my mother-in-law, who also "does keto," declared to my wife and me that she'd be enjoying one peanut M&M per day. Now, her diligence in maintaining her diet may seem extreme, but this daily allowance of a single peanut M&M allowed her to both enjoy a small amount of carbohydrates and sugar while also maintaining her body's ketosis.

37. Matt 5:28.

I believe(d) the lie that this dieting mentality could also work for lust. I thought small amounts of lust wouldn't result in problems. I believed no one would be hurt by me looking at other women, taking short peeks at pornography, or engaging in brief sexual fantasies. It could always be worse, right? Sure, I guess.

Lusting after a woman is probably better than actually committing physical adultery. Using pornography for five minutes is probably better than using for five hours. But these behaviors still aren't appropriate. My actions are contrary to what the Bible prescribes for righteous living. I sin against both God and myself when I lust.[38] I degrade those I'm lusting after because I'm objectifying them, even when it's "just a bit." Although the former actions may have, at least seemingly, lesser consequences than the latter actions, lust in any amount is unhealthy and unacceptable.

Line Up, Ladies!

Lust is also a manipulation machine. One cog in the machine is pornography, which convinces its users that women always want sex, even when they act or insist otherwise. Pornography creates the illusion that women are just waiting to be seduced.

When you pass a woman on the street, she wants you to make a sexual comment. If a woman smiles at you, she wants to perform oral sex on you. Each and every woman you encounter is just waiting to strip down and have sex with you. Or that's what lust and pornography would have you believe.

For me, lust and pornography had me convinced that women weren't people. They weren't God's glorious creations. They were mere objects, sexual parts for my enjoyment.[39]

This is the lie of objectification—the belief that human beings are mere commodities. Admitting I believed this lie is painful. Admitting I sometimes still believe this lie is shameful. God help me.

38. Exod 20:14 (cf. Matt 5:28); 1 Cor 6:18.
39. Struthers, *Wired for Intimacy*, 71.

To everyone reading this: You are *not* an object. You *deserve* to be treated with great honor, respect, and care. You *have* worth far beyond your sexual organs. You *are* God's child. We must stop treating people like objects.

Unfortunately, the statistics indicate that objectification isn't going away. Nearly half of teenagers and young adults use pornography.[40] If pornography implies that women always want sex, we shouldn't be surprised that people (both young and old) persist sexually even when their partner says or acts otherwise. God help us.

My Greatest Need

I'm drawn to entertainment that portrays varied dystopian futures. Reading or watching people engage their basic need for survival is refreshing. There's no time to worry about how many followers you have on social media when the world is collapsing around you.

Our basic needs are water, food, sleep, and shelter. We really don't *need* much to survive. Notice I didn't include sex in humanity's survival list. Unlike Johnny and Sally Caveman, we no longer *need* sex to survive.

Some will disagree with this statement, citing Abraham Maslow's 1943 essay "A Theory of Human Motivation," which posits five different levels of motivation humans move through when making decisions. The basest level is physiological, which seems to include sex. However, Maslow identifies physiological needs as necessary conditions for a body's basic functioning.[41] In other words, if I don't meet a physiological need, my body will not properly function. Sex doesn't meet that criterion; our bodies *can* function basically without sex.

Unfortunately, I was convinced otherwise. I believed the lie that sex *was* a *need*. In fact, it was my *greatest* need.[42] I often denied

40. Barna Group and Josh McDowell Ministry, *Porn Phenomenon*, 23.

41. A *necessary condition* states that "without *x*, you can't have *y*."

42. Struthers, *Wired for Intimacy*, 57. See also Carnes, *Out of the Shadows*, 16.

a real need (e.g., sleep) to pursue a pseudo-need (e.g., lust). To sleep, which meant denying my lust, would be like death.[43]

But the truth is that sex is not my greatest need. I won't die when I deny a sexual impulse (even a healthy impulse, like sex with my wife). I don't have to lust or use pornography to meet this so-called need. On the contrary, improved emotional, physical, and spiritual health has been a result of funneling my sexual energy towards my wife alone.

Rejection and Acceptance

If two cars are moving towards each other along a narrow street, both drivers must employ constant attention and careful navigation. They must both be willing participants for their mutual safety. If either driver decides to ignore their situation, the result could be disastrous.

Marriage (and most other relationships) is a lot like this. It requires constant attention, careful navigation, and willing participants. If these requirements are ignored, the result is often strained, or perhaps destroyed, relationships.

My wife attends to, navigates through, and participates in my emotional, physical, and spiritual needs when we are sexual. Now, that's not the *only* way these needs are met, but it is *one* way. And I sometimes still struggle with feeling rejected when she declines me sexually.

In the past, my normal was feeling rejected when my former wife declined sex. Although I don't believe she was trying to make me feel rejected when she declined, my emotional baggage created these feelings of rejection. Part of my emotional baggage came from almost always being the "third wheel" or "odd man out." I was always looking in from the outside, which affected my self-esteem. Although the cognitive truth is that God *is* enough for me, try saying that to a teenager who doesn't feel valued by other people. For young people, the intangibility of God can present problems to their

43. Carnes, *Out of the Shadows*, 27.

believing certain propositions as true (e.g., God is enough for you) when they don't tangibly experience these true propositions.

For me, these feelings left me starving for acceptance. My starvation prompted a seemingly never-ending search for something (e.g., pornography) or, eventually, someone (e.g., other women) that didn't make me *feel* rejected. Of course, I never felt rejected by lust or pornography because they never told me "no." I always *felt* attractive, wanted, and valued.[44] I always *felt* accepted. So, searching for these means of acceptance soon became easier than facing the prospective sexual rejection from my fomer wife.

But of course, I wasn't really accepted, wanted, or valued. Lust and pornography aren't great mistresses. I was still alone.[45] In fact, the more I pulled away from what *is* real—God, human relationships, myself—to pursue lust's false reality, the more lonely I became.

I once attended a small group with some friends while in college. Attending this small group, even just once, was an opportunity to pursue something real. Real relationships, with real friends, who really cared about me. Unfortunately, I spent my evening somewhere else. Although I was physically present, I was emotionally, mentally, and spiritually distant. My energy was instead spent thinking about returning home to use pornography to act out. I remember leaving as soon as possible.

True or False

Is the second premise true? Do lust's lies harm our "hearts"? The first premise (e.g., lust harms our brains) is largely scientific, however science cannot *prove* that lust harms our "hearts." There are reports by psychologists that using pornography (which involves lusting) makes relationships less stable and increases the likelihood of both infidelity and divorce. However, the truth of this

---

44. Wilson, *Your Brain on Porn*, 20.
45. Wilson, *Your Brain on Porn* , xv.

second premise is largely anecdotal.[46] Said in a different way, its truth rests on *my* experiences. You may doubt my experiences. You may not believe the lies I identified could be such heavy influencers. You may consider me a weak Christian because I was susceptible to these lies. Nevertheless, denying someone's personal experience is difficult, if not impossible. So the truth of premise two seems at least as likely as not.

Relationship Harm

Now comes the third premise: Lust harms our relationships. As a flawed human being, harming relationships is my common reality. Sometimes the harm is minimal, but I'm certainly capable of applying maximum harm to personal relationships.

The relational harm wrought by lust, pornography use, and adultery is difficult to manage. Fully experiencing the effects of lust's harm may take years. That is, I may not yet know the extent to which my struggle with lust, pornography use, and adultery has had on my personal relations with others. As such, I will focus on two specific relationships that have been harmed by my lust, pornography use, and adultery: my former wife and my daughter.[47]

Finalizing our divorce in January 2016 was the culmination of the relational harm wrought by my adultery, pornography use, and obsession with lust. But the relational harm didn't begin there. Our relationship—a marriage—had been deteriorating for years.

And although divorce may not be God's *ideal*, I can't blame her for divorcing me. *I* broke our marriage covenant; she did not. *I* was unfaithful; she was not. And *I* also eventually stopped fighting for our marriage.

Now, I'm not saying marriages aren't worth fighting for. They are. If you find yourself in a marriage, or other relationship, that is hurting, please continue fighting for as long as you're able. But relationships are like investing. When both parties invest,

46. Fight the New Drug, "How Porn Kills Love."
47. Struthers, *Wired for Intimacy*, 46, 58.

the return is high. This means you have much more to reinvest during good times, as well as savings to rely on when times are tough. However, once one party stops investing, your returns become smaller and the other party eventually depletes the relational savings until there's nothing left to invest. This is what happened in our relationship.

I don't know exactly when my former wife decided to give up investing in our marriage relationship, but I do remember when she told me that she would no longer be investing in our marital reconciliation. And I'm not trying to slander her here. To her credit, she has never treated me poorly. She has neither slandered me nor tried to drive a wedge between my daughter and me despite the great pain and turmoil I brought into our lives. I am not entitled to her kindness, but I'm grateful nonetheless. Nevertheless, as the investment in our marriage dwindled, I eventually had nothing left to invest. It just is what it is.

Now, we continue to work hard to foster a healthy and supportive co-parenting environment for our daughter despite our broken relationship. And yet, ignoring how my lust, pornography use, and adultery has harmed our relationship would be silly. Our relationship is not what it ought to be. It may never be. My hope is that she sees a changed person and forgives me for the pain and destruction I brought into our lives. All I can do is trust God to decrease her pain while increasing her joy by healing her heart and mind.

Unfortunately, this relationship isn't the only one I've harmed. Although I'm trying to be a good father, I know my lust, pornography use, and adultery has harmed my relationship with my daughter. I'll never forget the look on her face when we first told her I was moving out. Her little faced was contorted in such confused pain. This will always haunt my memories. This is the saddest moment of my life. It still hurts, even now.

During our divorce proceedings, we agreed on joint physical custody. For us, this means our daughter spends equal time with both biological parents. We believe having our daughter spend a few days each week at both homes is the best option for maintaining a healthy and supportive environment. But every time she leaves I'm reminded of my actions—lusting, using pornography, and committing adultery—that now prevent me from spending a maximum amount of time with her. Although I've come to cognitively accept this as a consequence of my actions, it's still heartbreaking. It just hurts so much.

Like I said earlier, I may not be able to fully recognize the total impact my lust, pornography use, and adultery has had on my relationships for some time. Maybe the pain is still too fresh? Maybe I've not yet adequately dealt with my sadness, guilt, and shame? Maybe there will be more to write later.

So what do you think of my argument? Do you think it's cogent? Are the premises true? For me, trying to avoid or deny the harm lust does to our brains, hearts, and relationships seems unwise. The correlation between brain science and emerging addiction studies seems difficult to ignore. And although the truth of premises two and three is largely anecdotal, identifying the lies we believe and the relationships we've harmed is a test of personal honesty. Unfortunately, long-term recovery isn't a result of simply acknowledging the cogency of this argument. Instead, the journey of recovery is often a long, lonely, and imperfect road. My journey has been longer, lonelier, and more imperfect than planned. But I am hopeful (and you can be too!).

6

From Relapse to Recovery

From Relapse . . .

THOSE IN THE RECOVERY community identify a loss of sobriety as a "relapse." To lose one's sobriety may mean returning to gambling or binge-eating, to using opiates or pornography. Most recovering from addiction(s), obsession(s), or compulsive behavior(s) relapse at some point, although there are some that never relapse after achieving initial sobriety. But they're the exception, not the rule.

What constitutes a relapse is different for each person. For those specifically obsessed with lust, addicted to using pornography, or some other compulsive sexual behavior, we may consider ourselves to have relapsed if we lust after a passerby, use pornography just once, or have another emotional or physical affair. The definition of a relapse varies from the *seemingly* harmless (e.g., lusting after the passerby or using pornography just once) to the *obviously* destructive (e.g., having another emotional or physical affair).

Again, my intent is *not* to excuse unhealthy sexual behaviors (mine or others). Rather, I want to help you understand that recovery is a journey, often long, lonely, and imperfect. Those recovering will likely relapse—to some extent at some point—despite our best intentions. Unfortunately, I'm not one the aforementioned exceptions. I've relapsed many times since first confessing my initial physical adultery to my former wife (see chapter 1).

Giving Up

I first confessed to my former wife about my initial physical adultery within hours of it happening. My confession in October 2013 was followed by eight months of decent sobriety. During these eight months, I neither used pornography nor had an emotional or physical affair. However, I began relapsing the following summer.

From an outsider's perspective, I probably appeared to be working hard to save my marriage. In many ways, I was. I went to individual therapy and a recovery group, as well as read various recovery-based materials. My former wife and I also occasionally saw a marriage counselor and tried being part of a local church family. Overall, we seemed to be progressing with our marriage's restoration. However, my secret relapses began subverting the progress we seemed to be making. By the summer of 2014, I had reverted back to regularly acting out to mental fantasy and occasional pornography use.

But don't be ignorant like I was. Acting out to mental fantasy will *never* be enough. Occasional pornography use will *never* remain occasional. These actions will *always* lead to something more. Maybe not right away, but they will eventually.

Then in May 2015, my former wife declared she wanted a separation. Although I had been hoping for the complete restoration of our marriage (despite my relapsing), I knew then that our marriage wasn't going to survive. It was disintegrating right before my eyes.

I retreated to our basement after she told me, curled into the fetal position, and despaired over my future. And then I snapped. The emotional, mental, physical, and spiritual toll became too much for me. So I gave up. I stopped trying to restore my marriage. I quit working on my recovery. I no longer cared. And lust, cunning and ruthless as ever, saw an opening to once again invade my hurting heart. And this time I didn't resist.

Picking Up Where I Left Off

When someone learns how to ride a bike, their brain should retain this "know-how" knowledge. That is, they should be able to pick up right where they left off, even if they haven't ridden a bike in years. An addict's brain operates in a similar way when they return to their substance or process (behavior). We don't need to be re-trained. We can pick up right where we left off.

At the end of chapter 1, I wrote that my real "rock bottom" came after my initial physical adultery. Unfortunately, I found a new low during the summer of 2015. During those few months my compulsive sexual behaviors reached depths I had not yet considered. Those were sad days; some of the saddest of my life.

. . . To Recovery

After much consideration, I've decided not to detail my 2015 relapse on these pages. In fact, although the original manuscript I submitted to the publisher did contain these details, I eventually asked to have it returned for an editing overhaul. Before we move to the section on my current recovery, I want to explain two reasons for this editing overhaul. And please know that this editing overhaul was a difficult decision for me. I don't want those who may have been connecting with my story to suddenly feel disconnected by what may seem to be avoidance or opaqueness.

My first reason is that once something has been published it can't become unpublished. Once it's out there, I can never make it not out there. Although I feel comfortable sharing parts of my story (like my initial physical adultery and developmental moments of pornography use), I'm not yet ready to share the details of my 2015 relapse. Maybe that will change one day; I'm not sure.

My second reason is that my daughter may read this book in the future. Although I desire to be honest, authentic, and transparent with my daughter (and most others for that matter), I'm not convinced she needs to know every specific detail of her father's sexual history. Maybe I'm wrong about that, but this is where I'm at (at least for now).

Sobriety Defined

Progress not perfection. Since 2015, this recovery mantra has encouraged me towards ever-increasing progress, while also releasing me from the suffocating expectation of perfection. I'm far from perfect, but I've made excellent progress.

For me, being "sober" includes not using pornography and not masturbating to other types of sexually stimulating materials. These are the *minimum* behaviors to avoid. Of course, more destructive behaviors, like emotional and physical affairs, are also to be avoided.

Now, I'm not perfect, but I'm making progress. I'm working towards avoiding both harmful actions and attitudes. Thankfully, neuroplasticity works both ways. Although my brain can be trained to respond to negative stimuli, it also can be trained to respond to positive stimuli. And as my brain is trained to respond to positive stimuli, it will also learn to avoid negative stimuli.[1] So what am I doing to train my brain to respond to positive stimuli and avoid negative stimuli?

Intimacy with God

When packing my backpack for high school, I always made sure to place my Bible in front of other school books. Now, I didn't take my Bible to school because I was some kind of "super-Christian." I needed it for my high school's daily Bible class. But it could never go behind or under another school book; to do so would dishonor both God and the Bible.[2] I'm feeling similar pressure now. That is, I'm fighting the internal pressure to make

---

1. Wilson, *Your Brain on Porn*, x, 110. See also Struthers, *Wired for Intimacy*, 87.

2. See chapter 2 of Svendsen's *Fundamentalist* for some similar situations.

sure "Intimacy with God" is designated as my *first* recovery tool, because to do otherwise would dishonor God. There's no way I can designate "Stop Using Pornography" as my first recovery tool. If I do, I might as well place my Bible behind my English and science textbooks.

But the truth is that God is *not* dishonored when I place another book in front or on top of my Bible. He's not wringing his hands, hoping I lead this chapter with "Intimacy with God" over "Stop Using Pornography." God doesn't need me to pander to him. In fact, God doesn't *need* anything from me (or you).[3] Nevertheless, I'm still going to lead with "Intimacy with God" as my first recovery tool.

I'm also not interested in acting like I have some super-spiritual-better-than-yours relationship with God. My relationship with God will *always* need work. It will never be what it ought to be. But I'm beginning to understand that intimacy with God *is* foundational for *my* sustained recovery, which is why it got first billing.[4] Of course, this doesn't mean you can *only* experience recovery if you have a relationship with God. For me, though, my relationship with God is critical to my ongoing recovery *because* I am a Christian.

Part of my recovery journey, then, is learning *how* to have a healthy relationship with God.[5] Reigniting this relationship has primarily come through asking questions, new ways of praying, and community. I need something fresh. I was raised in the church and have a seminary degree. I understand the standard American Christian model for pursuing God. However, regular church attendance, having a daily "quiet time," and using ACTS (Adoration, Confession, Thanksgiving, and Supplication) as a prayer model was the same system I followed while also being obsessed with lust, addicted to using pornography, and committing emotional and physical adultery. Something needs to change.

3. Acts 17:25.
4. Struthers, *Wired for Intimacy*, 43, 106–7.
5. Struthers, *Wired for Intimacy*, 15.

Asking questions, especially about your faith or theology, can be quite scary. But we don't need to fear asking questions. We don't even need to fear doubting what we believe. In fact, asking questions about your theology or doubting your faith may actually fortify your beliefs. The most solid beliefs are those you continue to affirm even after passionate skepticism. Put differently, if the faith, theology, or beliefs you have crumble when you apply skeptical pressure, how solid were those beliefs in the first place?

And I'm not saying that using ACTS as a prayer model is always a terrible idea. God deserves our adoration and thanksgiving. If we confess our wrongdoings to each other, then we ought to confess them to God too. My daughter feels comfortable asking me for (lots of) things, so I should also feel comfortable asking my cosmic parent for things (although both my daughter and I shouldn't necessarily expect to receive whatever we've requested). But these new ways of praying—meditative and recitative—don't fit the standard American Christian model, so some may feel squeamish.

For me, meditative prayer includes focusing on certain words and phrases, reflecting on their meanings, and acknowledging my body's response to this focused reflection. For instance, I may focus on the phrase "God loves me." I then try to understand what this phrase means *for* me. What does it mean for God to love me? I also try to notice how my body responds to this reflection. Does my body respond in a positive or negative way? What does it mean if my chest feels full or my stomach is in knots while reflecting on what it means that God loves me?

And recitative prayer includes, well, recitation. Over the past few years, I've found various prayers to recite that have positively affected my recovery, such as the Third Step Prayer, Serenity Prayer, and Prayer of Release.[6] These methods of prayer have been and continue to be helpful in my spiritual recovery journey.

God has also used people to show himself to me. Although I found myself in some dysfunctional relationships and unhealthy church communities during my early recovery, God has given me a small community of people who demonstrate God's tangible

---

6. See Appendix B for a list of helpful prayers.

love and grace to me on a regular basis. I'm so grateful for this community because they help nurture my mind and heart towards accepting the cognitive and emotive reality that God loves me for me and wants intimacy with me.

Learning how to have a healthy relationship with God has been, and will probably continue to be, a slow process. Lust has corrupted my ability to be intimate with God. I've spent most of my life believing that God is not enough for me and his love for and acceptance of me is conditional. But I'm trying to trust that God is long-suffering, demonstrating steadfast patience as I work towards embracing the truth that he *is* enough for me *because* he loves and accepts me without condition.[7]

Cease and Desist

My next recovery tool is avoiding lust and not using pornography. These are important recovery tools. If I'm trying to avoid type 2 diabetes, I ought to resist a donut-only lifestyle. A donut-only lifestyle would produce a body overstimulated by high blood sugar. The same is true for lust and pornography use. That is, I need to avoid chronically overstimulating my brain and body with lust and pornography use.[8]

Millions of people over many millennia have survived without regular sugar consumption. Over-using sugar is a modern conception. We can also apply this to pornography use. That is, millions of people over many millennia have survived without regular pornography consumption. We can too.[9]

In fact, our brains need rest from artificial sexual stimulation. However, our well-worn neural pathways may take months, even years, before they fire less.[10] Remember: Neurons that fire together wire together. Put differently, my neural wiring will only weaken

7. Struthers, *Wired for Intimacy*, 43. Exod 34:6; Pss 36:5; 52:8b; 86:15; 136; Jer 31:3; Joel 2:13; John 3:16; 2 Pet 3:9; 1 John 4:7–8.

8. Wilson, *Your Brain on Porn*, 87, 96.

9. Wilson, *Your Brain on Porn*, 151.

10. Wilson, *Your Brain on Porn* , 98–99.

as my neurons fire less. As I continue to work towards abstaining from lust and pornography use, my impulses towards and cravings for lust and pornography use diminish.

Also, *only* avoiding pornography use is not enough. If I advised a heroin addict to just use less heroin, or an alcoholic to switch to light beer, you should question my counsel. For me, reverting to "non-pornographic" images for lust and masturbatory purposes is analogous. Reductions in quantity or potency will not help the (drug, alcohol, pornography, etc.) user overcome their obsession, addiction, or compulsive behavior.

This also includes masturbating to mental fantasy. Any type of mental sexual fantasy could reactivate formerly wired neural circuits. And, in fact, these circuits *want* to be reactivated.[11] Don't forget that the activation of these circuits is an ancient survival mechanism.

Recovery is not necessarily an easy road to travel. It's going to take hard work. Thankfully, though, aids have been created to help those struggling with lust obsession and pornography (over)use.

Filters (. . . Aren't the Point)

My daughter sometimes requests a large bandage for a small scrape that's not even bleeding. When I try explaining to her that a bandage is meant to cover an open, bleeding wound, she responds by increasing the volume of her request. I know her request is silly because she doesn't need a large bandage for a small, non-bleeding scrape. But it also seems silly to consider a request for an opposite situation—requesting a tiny bandage to cover a large, gaping wound.

For some time, I used Internet filters and accountability software as tiny bandages to cover my large, gaping wounds of lie-fueled compulsive sexual behavior. Now I'm not saying Internet filters and accountability software aren't helpful. They are. Please

11. Wilson, *Your Brain on Porn*, 101, 136.

use them.[12] However, if we place all our hope for sustained recovery into these resources, we will likely fail. True healing requires our wound(s) to be scraped, cleaned, and properly bandaged. Simply placing a tiny bandage of Internet filters and accountability software over the gaping wound of addiction and compulsive sexual behavior will cause the wound to go untreated, likely festering into something far worse than you had planned. With God's help, I'm learning to identify, scrape, clean, and bandage my deep emotional wounds through healthy community, recovery groups, and individual therapy. All while still using whatever filters and software I can to help me along the way.

Individual Therapy

Someone once told me they were unwilling to pursue individual therapy because it would be too painful and, because of their increasing age, didn't consider it a worthwhile emotional investment. My heart still hurts when I think about this. I'm not going to deny the emotional, mental, and spiritual pain this person may experience in therapy, but they're already experiencing this pain. Isn't the mere possibility of resolving this pain worth it? Instead of trying to bury or stifle our pain (which definitely won't allow for healing to take place), we can open ourselves to the help offered by those with the academic and professional qualifications to teach healthy coping mechanisms. I hope this person (and all people) will one day see individual therapy as a worthwhile emotional investment because it's a safe place to process past pain and present emotions.

Therapy is not *only* for "crazy" people. This stigma needs to be left behind. Or, perhaps better put, we're all "crazy." We all have "issues." We should all be seeing a therapist. The collective emotional, mental, and spiritual health of our world would be far better if we all learned to cope in healthy ways. So why not seek the help of a professional?

12. Wilson, *Your Brain on Porn*, 103. See the bibliography and appendices for helpful resources!

Would you not speak with a lawyer if you needed legal counsel? Would you not seek the help of an obstetrician if you were pregnant? Would you not consult a cardiologist if you had heart problems? Of course, the answer is "yes." In fact, needing legal or medical help and *not* consulting a professional would be strange. So why is seeking the professional help of a psychologist/therapist/ counselor different? Again, *not* seeking help from someone trained to assist others in processing and managing their emotions and behaviors in a healthy manner is what seems strange.

And I realize some consider psychology, or therapy, to be anti-Christ. However, actuality does not necessarily follow from possibility. That is, the *possibility* of psychology being anti-Christ does not necessitate its *actuality*. Those concerned that psychology is anti-Christ, and therein detrimental to people's souls, are understandably worried that the Bible and its principles will be replaced with "secular" principles. For instance, many Christians believe we should fear the phrase "self-esteem." But can we develop a healthy understanding of self-esteem while also avoiding being anti-Christ? I think so.

Self-esteem can be understood as an outworking of our self-worth. As such, the crux is *how* we build our self-worth. And for human beings, our self-worth can be built upon being God's image-bearers[13] How could this *not* promote a healthy sense of self-worth? The only other being that shares God's likeness is Christ Jesus![14] Now, I'm not God, I'm far from perfect, and I sin more than I'd like; nevertheless, my self-esteem, which is based on my self-worth, is a direct result of bearing God's image.

I'm also not saying the *only* counsel to seek is from your psychologist/therapist/counselor. You may be helped after sharing your emotions and struggles with family, friends, or church leaders. But those struggling with addictive and compulsive sexual behaviors need to proceed with caution. A strong stigma of shame and disgust exists towards those struggling with lust, pornography use, or some other form of "deviant" sexual behavior.

13. Gen 1:26–27; 5:1–2; 9:6; Jas 3:9.

14. 2 Cor 4:4; Col 1:15.

More often than not, family, friends, and church leaders are *not* equipped (neither educationally *nor* personally) to handle knowing about your emotions and struggles, especially when related to your sexuality. They may be struggling to handle their *own* emotions and personal struggles. Unless family, friends, or church leaders are trained in brain science, human emotion, and addiction, you should first seek help from a psychologist/therapist/counselor for your "issues."

I've been seeing my therapist since December 2013. Individual therapy has been vital to my recovery. My therapist, an educated, practiced, and God-loving man, provides regular opportunities for me to think through my emotions and struggles. In fact, I've begun working through issues that would've remained otherwise unnoticed or not admitted. The therapeutic process has solidified some things I already knew about myself and taught me other things I never considered. For instance, I'm codependent.[15] Until recently, I wouldn't have even understood what that means. But now I've been able to identify that part of my codependency includes obsessing over meeting other's expectations, and that connecting with my own independent thoughts and feelings will help me become the healthiest version of me.

Also, you may be wondering about the efficacy of individual therapy. Some critics will likely think, "If individual therapy is so great, then how could you relapse several years later? Individual therapy must be inept!" Again, possibility doesn't necessitate actuality. *I* chose to reject the biblical, practical, and therapeutic advice given to me. *I* chose to no longer maintain honest, humble, and transparent relationships with my therapist, sponsor, and recovery group. *I* am to blame, *not* my therapist or therapeutic principles.

Recovery Groups

Biological family bonds are important. However, other types of family-like bonds can be important too. For me, certain friendships

---

15. Go to http://coda.org to see if you are codependent.

and groups of people have been just as familial as my blood relatives. Recovery groups are one such instance.

Being around others who share your general, and sometimes particular, struggle(s) is a great relief.[16] I was terrified walking into my first recovery group meeting. My mind was filled with questions like: What am I admitting if I enter that room? Who really am I? Do I have the same problems as these people? But what began as fear evolved into love. These people who are part of my recovery groups are now also my family.

One recovery group I attend will remain nameless, because they're an "anonymous" group.[17] However, the other recovery group I attend is not anonymous. Celebrate Recovery is a ministry founded and facilitated by Saddleback Church.[18] As a Christian, the overt Christ-centered ethos of Celebrate Recovery is endearing. Each week my Celebrate Recovery group begins with a communal dinner, which is followed by singing and either reviewing a recovery principle or hearing a personal testimony. We then split into smaller, gender- and recovery-specific groups for discussion and accountability before ending the evening with a communal dessert. For those attending Celebrate Recovery, relating to one another, or "doing community," is just as crucial as the discipline of confession and accountability.

Of course, receiving individual therapy or attending recovery groups doesn't guarantee lasting recovery. These things are not magic pills. I could attend both individual therapy and recovery groups without experiencing lasting change. In fact, I did for some time during those difficult months in 2015. As such, individual therapy and recovery groups need to be seen as tools to help identify, scrape, clean, and bandage my emotional, mental, and spiritual wounds. They are a means to an end, not ends themselves.

---

16. Wilson, *Your Brain on Porn*, 105–6.

17. See Appendix A for "anonymous" recovery groups!

18. http://www.celebraterecovery.com.

Trigger Happy

A trigger can be understood as any factor, either external or internal, that makes me want to lust.[19] External factors can be, amongst other things, television and movies, sexually explicit language, or even getting into my car (see chapter 2). Internal factors, or states of mind, include, amongst other things, being hungry, angry, lonely, or tired.[20] We may share some similar triggers, but are unlikely to share all the same triggers.[21] Most triggers will be unique to our own experiences.

We can think of triggers as "cues."[22] When cued, an actor should give their line. When cued, an addict probably acts out. The ritualization process identified in chapter 2 often involves triggers. The neural pathways in my brain received a jolt of electrical activity every time I got into my car, which then compelled me to troll for sex workers. This jolt fed my "need" to lust, which often felt like a matter of life and death.[23]

Undoing the trigger of getting into my car has been a long process. In fact, it can still be a trigger. Again, neurons that fire together wire together.[24] I also have many other negative triggers to identify and undo.[25] Some triggers are obvious and easily identified, such as seeing an attractive woman or being alone. But other triggers are less obvious. These triggers often require serious introspection (often with the assistance of individual therapy or recovery groups) to be identified. Once identified, I can then work towards placing myself into a cautious state.[26] My sponsor calls it "defensive driving." If I can understand what's happening to my

19. Wilson, *Your Brain on Porn*, 124.

20. Wilson, *Your Brain on Porn*, 125.

21. Wilson, *Your Brain on Porn*, 125.

22. Wilson, *Your Brain on Porn*, 126.

23. Wilson, *Your Brain on Porn*, 126.

24. Wilson, *Your Brain on Porn*, 68.

25. To be fair, triggers are not only and always problematic. Positive triggers can be helpful.

26. Wilson, *Your Brain on Porn*, 125.

brain when I'm triggered, I can then help myself by asking honest ("defensive driving") questions like:

- What is my current situation?
- What am I feeling?
- Who can I reach out to for help?
- What do I need right now to "work my program"?

Working My Program

Speaking of working my program, this has become an ever-increasing crucial part of my recovery journey. For me, working my program involves following these Twelve Steps:

1. We admitted that we are powerless over lust—that our lives have become unmanageable.

2. We came to believe that a Power greater than ourselves could restore us to sanity.

3. We made the decision to turn our will and our lives over to the care of God.

4. We made a searching and fearless moral inventory of ourselves.

5. We admitted to God, to ourselves, and to another human being the exact nature of our wrongs.

6. We were entirely ready to have God remove all these defects of character.

7. We humbly asked him to remove our shortcomings.

8. We made a list of all persons we had harmed, and became willing to make amends to them all.

9. We made direct amends to such people wherever possible, except when to do so would injure them or others.

10. We continued to take personal inventory and when wrong, promptly admit it.

11. We sought through prayer and meditation to improve our conscious contact with God, praying for knowledge of his will for us and the power to carry that out.

12. We try to carry this message to others, and to practice these principles in all our affairs.

As you can see, step 12 instructs me to carry my message of recovery to others. Having worked steps 2 and 3 (i.e., turning my life and will over to Christ Jesus after coming to believe that he could restore my sanity), I can now carry my strength, experience, and hope to others struggling with similar obsessions, addictions, and compulsive behaviors. So how am I working step 12?

God often exceeds our expectations. In the midst of my 2015 relapse, God used a trip to Uganda to both refresh my soul and give me an opportunity to begin working step 12. My soul was refreshed after speaking with a pastor from Kentucky who listened well and extended grace to me in a way I'd yet experienced. He did not shame me or manipulate me with guilt. He did not use fear as a tool for emotional blackmail. He just listened and shared in my sorrow over my struggles.

This incredibly meaningful experience was bested only by be-friending a local Ugandan man. He was employed by the organiza-tion we were serving, and his work space was in the same area as my own. We spent many hours talking about our respective cultures as well as various spiritual matters, always trying to sprinkle as much humor into our conversations as possible. Our personalities clicked. Towards the end of my time in Uganda, I couldn't shake the feeling that he was the real reason why I'd come to Africa.

We decided to exchange contact information before I left, and communicated sporadically for the next few months. Eventually, he began asking probing questions about my dissolving marriage. He already knew my former wife had filed for divorce, so I decided to tell him the rest of my story. Now, this book isn't an exposé on this man. It's enough to say that we share some similar struggles, which we began working through together after sharing my story with him.

We have become fast and dear friends since first meeting in the Ugandan "bush." I try to travel to Uganda every year to encourage him by continuing to share my experience, strength, and hope with him because he doesn't have access to the same resources as I do (e.g., individual therapy, recovery groups, etc.), so I'm resolved to help him in any way possible. We also both believe we have roles to play in bringing awareness to the deeply embedded culture of lust and pornography use ensnaring Ugandans.

I'm also working step 12 by writing this book. I once spoke with Seth Taylor,[27] who encouraged me to finish writing and then "release it." So that's what I'm doing. I'm releasing this book to you, hoping my story affects you and anyone else who reads this book.

But I knew writing this book would be a therapeutic project for me, even if it was never published. I knew it needed to be completed. The writing process has helped me consider my past, better understand how my brain works, recognize how my attitudes and actions hurt others, and solidify my burden to help others struggling with similar issues.

I also want to work step 12 by speaking with people about my experience, strength, and hope. I have recently started working towards a graduate degree in clinical mental health counseling because I know people are hiding, full of fear, shame, and guilt. If this is you, please know you're not alone. There is hope. You can be free of fear, shame, and guilt.

But be warned: *You* must want recovery. You have to work your program. No one else can want recovery or work your program for you. My sponsor was brilliant by *not* pressuring me to change. Although he remained close emotionally and spiritually during my 2015 relapse, he waited for *me* to decide that *I* wanted to live a life of hope and healing.

I'm trying to employ this same mindset with others. Regardless of what someone may be struggling with, people won't change until they're ready. You can't force change upon people. In the many instances when I wasn't yet ready to change, I would simply alter my lifestyle until the person trying to force my changed behavior

---

27. Go read his *Feels Like Redemption*.

backed off. And once they backed off I would then continue my addictive and sexually compulsive attitudes and actions.

And trust me, I understand; wanting recovery can be difficult. Admitting your faults and failures is scary. Right now you may not even be able to admit your obsession with lust, pornography use, fornication, adultery, voyeurism, exhibitionism, solicitation, sex work, etc. because of the fear, shame, and guilt you feel. For decades, lust lied to me about not being able to talk to others about my obsession with lust, pornography use, and compulsive sexual behavior.

Secrets, Secrets Are No Fun. Secrets, Secrets Hurt Someone.

If I tell another person about my struggle(s), they will reject me. My only choice is to stay silent and isolate myself from others. This lie, which I believed for decades, creates an ever-darkening chasm in which the addict wallows. Guilt, shame, and fear perpetuate in the chasm of silence and isolation, which keeps their obsession(s), addiction(s), or compulsive behavior(s) in the dark to fester and grow.

Like I said in chapter 2, I often wonder about those around me who may be ensnared by lust and pornography use, especially within Christian contexts. These people are likely terrified that someone will discover their secret. And their fear is often validated by the church. For too long the church has helped perpetuate the lie that talking plainly about lust, pornography, sex, etc. is dirty. For too long the church has heaped unnecessary guilt and shame upon those struggling with obsessions, addictions, and compulsive behaviors. For too long the church has avoided issues of mental health. So then, we now turn to the final chapter of this book, where I address certain concerns about how the church interacts with those struggling with obsessions, addictions, and compulsive behaviors. I also hope to offer some insight into how the church can better help me, and others like me who may also be struggling with obsessions, addictions, or compulsive behaviors.

7

Lust and the Church

LUST IS RAMPANT, PORNOGRAPHY use is excessive, and addiction is growing. Whether male or female, young or old, rich or poor, we have all been shaped by these issues. And the church has not gone unaffected.

My burden is primarily for the church. I long to see healing amongst God's people, which can be facilitated by changing church culture. The inconsistency of the church in addressing sin is unsettling. We are quick to judge lust, but slow to condemn pride. We resist challenging greed, but denigrate the adulterer. We overlook abuses of power, but show disgust towards sexual sin.

We should not be surprised then that those struggling with lust, pornography use, or adultery avoid identifying themselves within the church. Those struggling may recognize (at least outwardly) the harmfulness of lust, pornography use, and adultery, but the stigmas surrounding these behaviors dissuade them from getting the help they need. And even when someone struggling with addiction to lust, pornography use, or adultery does finally speak up, others often presuppose the following:

- "Your lust is much more sinful than my x (where x is their sin issue)."
- "If you use pornography, you must also prey on children."
- "If you're an adulterer, you must also be a rapist."

These stigmatic statements are not only largely untrue, but also promote an unhealthy sense of fear, guilt, and shame, which keeps addicts isolated and prevents them from seeking the help they need. If "soul care" is your profession (e.g., clergy), your church needs you to either become educated about human brains and emotions, or release those struggling to mental health professionals.[1] Unfortunately, clergy (including non-professional clergy) are often ill-equipped to help those with cognitive and emotional issues.

To be fair, I'm not convinced clergy *are* responsible for educating themselves about human brains and emotions. A lawyer may be proficient in other academic disciplines, but their *responsibility* is to know the law. Likewise, clergy may be proficient in psychology or counseling, but their *responsibility* is to know the Bible and theology.[2]

Of course, both the Bible and theology speak about the church, which is made up of humans who have brains and emotions. Perhaps the solution is to release those struggling with lust, pornography use, or adultery to mental health professionals, while maintaining a safe and healthy environment of biblical and theological encouragement for those struggling with lust, pornography use, or adultery. One way the church can cultivate such an environment is to understand the potential negative impact of fear, guilt, and shame, which often results in isolation as a result of spiritual abuse.[3]

Fear

Within the first few months of 2018, there were more than a dozen shootings on school campuses. As a father to a school-aged child, this has produced fear in me. Fear can be understood as an emotional response to a perceived threat or danger. Thankfully, a

1. Struthers, *Wired for Intimacy*, 14. See also Wilson, *Your Brain on Porn*, xvi, 94, 134.

2. Lewis, *Mere Christianity*, 83.

3. DeSilva, *Honor, Patronage, Kinship & Purity*, 90.

shooting on my daughter's elementary school campus has not yet happened, but it could. In this instance, my fear is actually helpful because it produces parental vigilance. As such, fear is not an emotion to necessarily avoid.

From a Christian perspective, the Bible refers to fear in different ways. On one hand, we are to fear God. On the other hand, we are not to live in fear.[4] So how should we approach fear?

Fearing God is complex, but should result from understanding his power. Some biblical references instruct us to demonstrate respectful reverence towards God.[5] This really isn't that strange. The bravest adventurer should demonstrate respectful reverence towards the ocean when kayaking through a hurricane. As the ocean's creator, God's might far surpasses the most powerful ocean wave. Therefore, if God is omnipotent (i.e., all-powerful), then he deserves our respectful reverence.

Other biblical references instruct people to fear (i.e., have an emotional response to) falling into the hands of the living God (i.e., a perceived threat or danger) *because* he can punish sin and, therefore, may not be safe.[6] In C. S. Lewis's *The Lion, the Witch, and the Wardrobe*, Mr. Beaver indicates Aslan is not safe (i.e., he's dangerous), but he is good.[7] Most consider Aslan to be Lewis's image of Christ Jesus (i.e., God). So God isn't necessarily safe, but he is good.

I fear both God's punishment and abandonment. Now, fearing God's punishment of sinful attitudes and actions isn't problematic. However, fearing God's abandonment is problematic.

Most would consider me a poor parent if I didn't punish my daughter's bad behavior. However, punishment should not be analogous to abandonment. Although my daughter may face punishment for bad behavior, she should *never* face abandonment. Regardless of her actions, I should *always* extend love and acceptance

---

4. Lam 3:57; 2 Tim 1:7; Heb 13:6.

5. Deut 6:24; Pss 31:19; 34:9; 128:4; 147:11; Prov 15:16; 19:23; Luke 1:50.

6. See Heb 10:31 and Luke 12:4–5, respectively.

7. Lewis, *The Lion, the Witch, and the Wardrobe*, 86.

to her. I hope to love my daughter and therefore treat her well no matter how she acts.

Those of us struggling with lust, pornography use, or adultery need to understand that God is love.[8] If I, as an imperfect parent, can love and treat my daughter well despite her bad behavior, how much more will an omnibenevolent (i.e., all-good) God love and treat his children?[9] We need not fear God's abandonment or mistreatment.[10] Doing so is a result of faulty core beliefs that God's love and acceptance are conditional.

Unfortunately, those of us struggling with lust, pornography use, or adultery often fear both God *and* people. We often fear the punishment, abandonment, and mistreatment of other people, despite the Bible's contrary instruction.[11] And, perhaps more unfortunately, our fear is sometimes validated.

I've been both mistreated and abandoned by some who know parts of my struggle with lust, pornography use, and adultery. As a direct result of their actions, I now fear others will also mistreat or abandon me for any future failings (sexual or otherwise). Maybe you have also been mistreated or abandoned because of your struggles. Or maybe you are hesitant to speak with someone because you fear being mistreated or abandoned. I can relate. Your fear is understandable. It can be so paralyzing, so immobilizing. Fear can harm our efforts to know, love, and serve God.[12]

But we don't have to be afraid. Jesus offers *his* peace.[13] And this peace cannot be overstated. It's literally God dwelling with(in) us! Therefore, even when others mistreat or abandon you, God never has or will.

8. 1 John 4:8.

9. Matt 7:11.

10. Deut 31:6; Rom 8:31–39; Heb 13:5.

11. Lam 3:57; 2 Tim 1:7; Heb 13:6.

12. Elwell and Beitzel, eds., *Baker Encyclopedia of the Bible*, 782.

13. John 14:27.

Guilt

I'm feeling guilt for having just eaten a double-chocolate brownie. Of course, eating dessert isn't inherently wrong; however, in this moment it sure feels that way. Eating a double-chocolate brownie feels wrong because it's full of sugar, and doesn't promote my physical health. Guilt is feeling regret or remorse when we've done, or want to do, something we believe is wrong (whether this thing *is* wrong is another issue).[14]

Now, we've all experienced guilt at some point. For addicts, though, guilt is a regular emotion, often residing within despair (the fourth stage of the addictive cycle). I empathize with King David when he wrote, "I know my transgressions, and my sin is always before me."[15] For instance, my daughter's custody situation is an ever-present reminder of my sin. Whether she's with me or with my former wife, my sinful past is part of what caused the dissolution of her nuclear family. I experience guilt every time I consider the pain she endures because of my sin. And yet, guilt is also not an emotion to necessarily avoid.

God can use guilt as a means to draw us to him. The apostle Paul mentions "godly sorrow," which could include the emotion of guilt, which could then bring repentance.[16] Of course, I may not respond appropriately to my guilt. I may attempt to cope with my guilt-ridden despair by returning to preoccupation (the first stage of the addictive cycle) instead of repenting. So how, or when, is guilt problematic?

Guilt is problematic when those within the church use unwarranted "guilt trips" to manipulate those struggling with lust, pornography use, or adultery. Manipulation doesn't promote mental health, and it's not pastoral. In fact, it's spiritual abuse. Unfortunately, those within the church may not even realize they're manipulating or spiritually abusing people. Nevertheless, ignorance should *never* excuse abuse.

14. Struthers, *Wired for Intimacy*, 56.

15. Ps 51:3.

16. 2 Cor 7:10. See also Struthers, *Wired for Intimacy*, 56.

Those within the church, especially its leaders, need to recognize their responsibility to shepherd people and, therefore, resist the power grab of manipulating people with "guilt trips." Using "guilt trips" to manipulate those of us struggling with lust, pornography use, or adultery to feel worse than we already do is never appropriate. Those who use "guilt trips" to manipulate others seem to want to establish an implicit claim that they have also been hurt. They may feel betrayed by this person's actions, or unworthy because this person didn't seek their help or counsel.

For Christians, whether we're experiencing "godly sorrow" or a manipulative "guilt trip," we can rest in the fact that our guilty status has been forever removed by the sacrificial atonement of Christ Jesus.[17] All we've done, all we're doing, and all we'll do has already been forgiven though Christ's death and resurrection.[18] God has forgiven sin, so we can release our guilt.[19]

However, guilt is not always based on external actions. Guilt can sometimes be found within internal thoughts and feelings. Of course, external actions can affect internal thoughts and feelings; however, internal thoughts and feelings, especially when directed towards the self, are often shame-based, not guilt-based.

Shame

Shame and guilt often go hand in hand. However, guilt results from bad behavior, whereas shame results from considering the self less valuable.[20] Put differently, guilt is about *doing*, while shame is about *being*.[21] As such, shame is far more dangerous than fear or guilt.

Shame, as a conduct guide, has been part of culture since ancient times. Honor codes were prevalent in Greco-Roman

17. Ps 103:12; Rom 8:1–2; 1 Pet 2:24.
18. 1 Pet 3:18.
19. Ps 51:1–2; 1 John 1:9.
20. Desilva, *Honor, Patronage, Kinship & Purity*, 25.
21. Struthers, *Wired for Intimacy*, 56.

society, as well as the far and near East.[22] For instance, an ancient citizen-soldier may continue fighting in a losing battle to avoid the shame of fleeing.

Similarly, you may deny an adulterous invitation because you wish to avoid the shame often attached to such actions. Shame, then, can be positive as it pushes us away from actions or behaviors that may induce this emotion.[23] So, along with fear and guilt, shame is also not an emotion to necessarily avoid.

Unfortunately, shame is often used in unhealthy or unwarranted ways. Unhealthy or unwarranted shame is attributed to the person *post* action. This type of shame often results in a certain "level of gnawing self-doubt, occasionally reaching the intensity of fully inflamed self-hatred."[24]

We hate who we've become because of what we've done. We hate who we are because of what we're doing. And so we believe others hate us too.

Now, despite the horror of self-hatred, we are, biblically speaking, sinful people.[25] We've fallen short of God's glory because we're spiritually corrupt.[26] However, a theological paradox exists, for we are both sinful and God's image-bearers. This seems to imply that shame-induced self-hatred denies the worth and value God places on his image-bearers.[27] In fact, New Testament scholar David deSilva believes unhealthy and unwarranted shame is "pathogenic . . . the kind of shame that the church should heal rather than reinforce."[28] One way to promote healing from unhealthy shame is for everyone to admit their own mistakes.[29] Why are we so afraid to admit we mess up?

22. Desilva, *Honor, Patronage, Kinship & Purity*, 23.

23. Desilva, *Honor, Patronage, Kinship & Purity*, 25. See also Karen, "Shame," 42, 58.

24. Karen, "Shame," 42, 58.

25. Gen 3:1–6; Ps 14:1–4; Eccl 7:20; Rom 3:9–18, 23; Eph 2:1; 1 John 1:8.

26. Rom 3:23.

27. Struthers, *Wired for Intimacy*, 56.

28. DeSilva, *Honor, Patronage, Kinship & Purity*, 90.

29. Matt 7:5; Luke 6:42.

To be sure, church leaders should lead by admitting their own failures (sexual or otherwise). Unfortunately, church leaders often exempt themselves from these admissions unless they're compelled to confess some major moral failure before resigning from active ministry. For the short time I was a pastor, I rarely talked to anyone about my struggle with lust and pornography use. Fear, guilt, and shame kept me isolated. Although I hated myself for these behaviors, my fear of active ministry disqualification due to sexual sin disclosure kept me quiet. And yet, had I been willing to actually admit my failings, they could have been identified and appropriately dealt with before becoming disqualifying. Everyone within the church, both its leaders and lay people, needs to recognize that no difference exists amongst us. We have all messed up. We all struggle with "stuff." We all have "issues."

For those of us struggling with lust, pornography use, or adultery, we need to embrace our identity as God's image-bearers.[30] And this doesn't mean we don't confront our own sin or use shame as a healthy deterrent for future poor choices. However, we can still acknowledge and embrace our worth and value found in Christ Jesus as we confront our sin. We need to reject self-hatred, embrace Christ Jesus, and live freely. Otherwise, you may be doomed to self-inflicted isolation, which keeps us from seeking the help we need.

Isolation

One of my favorite TV shows is *Alone*. This show follows ten survival experts as they live alone in the wilderness. These various experts bring ten survival items, and then compete against each other to see who can stay in the wilderness the longest.

Interestingly enough, many of these experts exit the challenge because the isolation becomes too much to handle. One contestant, participating in more than one season, is so talented that he built two log cabins (one for each season) with nothing more than

30. Struthers, *Wired for Intimacy*, 123.

an ax, saw, and other natural elements he found in the woods. And yet, he still ended up leaving the competition because he wanted to be around other people again. Now, I've not participated in a competition to test my mental fortitude against isolation, but I have still experienced my own extreme form of isolation because of my obsession with lust, addiction to pornography, and other compulsive sexual behaviors.

Isolation is often the result of not dealing with fear, guilt, and shame in healthy ways. Of course, periods of isolation are not necessarily problematic. As an introvert, I crave "alone time" (i.e., isolation). In fact, isolation can be an excellent spiritual discipline. Even Jesus withdrew sometimes to pray alone.[31] As such, isolating to "recharge" or seek God without distraction can be healthy. However, isolating because of fear, guilt, or shame is unhealthy. So, the question seems to be: *Why* are we isolating?

Unfortunately, addicts often isolate because of fear, guilt, or shame. And our isolation is not always physical. I spent much physical time with others while remaining emotionally, mentally, and spiritually isolated. I could not let anyone know the "real me." I could not let anyone discover my "problems." So I hid, isolating myself from everything, rather than turning towards that which could help—God and others. And with greater isolation came a deeper addictive hole.

Spiritual Abuse

What's worse is that unhealthy isolation can result from being pierced by the sharp arrows of fear, guilt, and shame, shot with the bow of spiritual abuse by those we ought to trust the most. Those we ought to trust—especially church leaders—are spiritually abusive when they use fear, guilt, and shame to manipulate those of us struggling with lust, pornography use, or other sexually compulsive behaviors. Unfortunately, spiritual abuse is becoming normal within churches. If you Google "spiritual abuse stories,"

31. Luke 5:16.

you will likely find a number of stories from people finally able and willing to share how they were spiritually abused by so-called righteous church leaders.

If you're a church leader, I'm pleading with you to recognize that instilling unwarranted fear, guilt, and shame is unhelpful and non-pastoral. In fact, *you* should feel guilty if you are berating, denigrating, or manipulating those trying to both recognize and share their struggles. The necessary bravery that addicts muster to both recognize and share their struggle(s) with another person is incomprehensible to the non-addict.

Unfortunately, those we often seek help from (e.g., our closest spiritual advisors) are either unable or unwilling.[32] Church leaders need to recognize that addiction (sexual or otherwise) is like pant size. Lots of people wear 36x32 pants, but each still has a unique fit. Others may find that size either too small or too large. One pant size does not fit all, and one way to think about or do recovery does not fit all. As a former pastor, I'm confident that most church leaders think *their* way is best. But, really, matters of brains, emotions, addictions, and recovery programs should be left with trained mental health professionals.

Now this doesn't mean church leaders shouldn't call addicts to repentance and righteous living. However, church leaders need to check their own attitudes, actions, and motivations because spiritual abuse is often the result of a manipulative power grab, where a church leader seeks feelings of superiority, power, and control.[33] This is not acceptable behavior. No rational person believes emotional, mental, or physical abuse to be acceptable under certain circumstances. Why would the same not be true for spiritual abuse? As such, spiritual abuse is also never acceptable.

I was spiritually abused by someone I once considered a friend and pastoral colleague. I came to this person, pouring out my heart, completely devastated by my 2015 relapse. After hearing my confession, this person responded to my disclosure by attempting to emotionally blackmail me. Now I'm fairly confident

---

32. See the bibliography and appendices for helpful resources!

33. Johnson, *Foundations for Soul Care*, 595.

this person does not think they were spiritually abusive. And yet, abusers don't get to qualify *what* abuse is or *who* has been abused. I'm not sure why this person deemed emotional blackmail the best response; perhaps this person was unable to handle the intensity of my disclosure, or maybe they felt pressure to control my situation or recovery, or this person's own "issues" may have clouded their judgment. Only this person really knows.

Regardless of the *why*, this person's attempted emotional blackmail was tantamount to both gossip and slander. Ironically, this person was so focused on bringing my sin to light that they couldn't see their own sin (e.g., gossip and slander).[34] This person could not, or would not, recognize that sharing sensitive information which had been given in confidence was inappropriate. Unfortunately, this person is still either unable or unwilling to admit their own sin and make amends to me. As a result, I no longer communicate with this person because I must protect my emotional, mental, and spiritual health. You may need to protect yourself from those who have spiritually abused you too. Setting healthy boundaries is a great first step.[35]

Also, for those of us who have been spiritually abused, we must remember that God loves us. He will not abuse, mistreat, or abandon us, despite how we may feel from our interactions with other people. Although we must seek mental health professionals and recovery communities for healing to occur, we can also find healing and recovery from any type of abuse in the person of Christ Jesus through the power of the Holy Spirit.[36]

On the Road Again

Whether you have fear or guilt, even if you've experienced shame or spiritual abuse, I'm pleading with you to not isolate yourself. God loves you without condition. There are others, both within

34. Lev 19:16; Prov 10:18; 11:13; 16:28; 20:19; Matt 7:5; Luke 6:42; Rom 1:29–30; Jas 1:26; 4:11.

35. You can start by reading Cloud and Townsend's *Boundaries*.

36. Struthers, *Wired for Intimacy*, 15.

and outside the church, that will accept you even in your struggles. If we look to God and others for help, we can find a healthy place for recovery and healing.

And so, this part of our journey together is ending. I'm so grateful for your investment in my journey by reading this book. By sharing my story I hope this book helps you understand you're not alone. By investigating brain science I hope this book helps you understand your struggles are not only spiritual. By talking about my recovery I hope this book helps you understand that healing can happen. By addressing the church I hope this book helps you understand that there are some who can help you in recovery, as well as some to avoid. I want so much for my story to give you hope. I want so much for you to finish this book encouraged. So keep reading. Although my time with you is ending, my wife has penned a humbling and encouraging *afterword*.

See you on the road.

Afterword

SAYING I'M PROUD OF my husband is a vast understatement. It also wouldn't tell the whole story.

I don't know about you, but I'm a big fan of stories. My mother read chapter books to my brother and me when we were very young, creating within us a love for reading and appreciation for storytelling. I relish getting lost in a good story—from meeting the characters, to the climax and resolution. My love of stories translates into an interest in other people's life stories—where we come from, how we got here, how all the details are woven together, the mystery of how it will end. It all *means* something. Everyone has a story. Some stories are filled with painful chapters we wish we could rip out, and most are filled with pages we wish to relive over and over again. My story has both. Some of it is difficult to reread. However, even in those dark chapters, I knew God's steady hand was writing my story. He was so evident to me in those times, so close to me. With his strength or by his grace, I kept putting one foot in front of the other, turning each page to see what it would hold.

By the time I met Dan, I had weathered a devastating divorce, and was hopeful for my future, settling into a happy single girl's life. I was grateful for the struggles I'd endured. God had used them to instill in me a dependence on him, and a new understanding of my worth and identity in Christ. I was beginning to grasp the fact that nothing could change his love for me or take away who I was in him. However, I didn't realize that the next season of my life would require more of this understanding than I could have known back then.

When Dan and I went on our first date, he shared his life story first. He didn't delve into the details of how or why his first marriage ended. It was only our first date, after all. My guess is most normal people would behave that way too. Dan talked about his upbringing, and we laughed about both attending Cornerstone Music Festival in our younger years. He gushed about his daughter, and never spoke an ill word about his ex-wife, praising her as a wonderful mother. The lingering pain from his divorce was still evident on his face despite the healing that had already taken place. I understood that pain, and my heart truly empathized with him. Divorce is a horrible experience, its wounds leaving scars that last a lifetime.

Later that evening, it was my turn to share. Being a chronic over-sharer, I told him all the painful steps that led to the end of my first marriage, including being a victim of my ex-husband's infidelity. While I saw myself as a survivor, I had been rescued by a powerful and loving God, and I wanted to make that known above all else. I walked out of that dark season of my life still in one piece only because of God's faithfulness and goodness to me. He is the loving Storywriter, and I believed he would redeem all my pain. Should I find love again, I knew that person would appreciate my story. So I bared it all, hoping to be truly heard, hoping he would get it.

Before Dan and I began dating, I had gone out with a few other guys who didn't seem interested in hearing my story. But this was different. Dan was different. He listened intently. And in his eyes I could see that he got it. It meant something to him. This was huge for me.

Our first date ended with some powdered donuts (a favorite of ours) and plans to see each other the following week. I felt like I was walking on air. I barely slept that night, and the next few days were a blur of happiness. Dan's sweet texts had me grinning nonstop. I couldn't explain it. Something just felt right.

But then, the morning before our next date, he texted me, asking to speak with me in person. He needed to disclose something important. He wanted to be completely honest with me.

The feeling of rightness immediately evaporated. My gut was telling me something I didn't want to believe. I wondered if something in my story had shaken an ugly secret loose. I drove to our neighborhood coffee shop with a huge, nervous pit in my stomach.

We sat in his car, awkwardly at first. He had brought a box of tissues, which didn't feel like a good sign. Then, without much hesitation, he began telling me the darker parts of his story, which had been omitted on our first date. There it was—the ugly truth. That thing my gut had been telling me . . . it was spot on. He had been unfaithful in his marriage.

I had yet to learn all the details. Some would come in time, and others wouldn't materialize until I read chapters of this book. But in that moment, faced with this information, I came to a crossroads. Did I want to continue dating him?

Dan didn't pressure me. He never has. He even used the words "no pressure" when he gave me his phone number and asked me out. He has a way of making me feel safe.

In fact, he strongly encouraged me to share what he told me with my close friends and family, to ask for prayer and advice, to take my time deciding whether I still wanted to pursue a relationship with him. I was floored. He wanted me to *tell* people? He wasn't asking me to hide this from those important to me? And even more so, *he* wasn't hiding his past? He was risking losing me for the sake of being honest. I had never experienced anything like this before. One on hand, I was even more impressed with him for his transparency. On the other hand, though, it felt like a sick joke, one that I felt like God was in on. Of all the guys on the planet, why was I beginning what felt like a perfect relationship with a man who had hurt his ex-wife the same way my ex-husband had hurt me? What were the odds? It felt like cosmic cruelty.

I used many of the tissues he brought. A confusing deluge of emotions washed over me. I was angry at the circumstances. I felt valued beyond measure. I already really liked him, so I was terrified that he had the potential to hurt me. It was overwhelming.

We parted ways, promising to reconnect later that evening. I didn't yet know if I would have an answer for him. I still wanted to go on our date the next day, but I felt hopeless about it actually happening. Our budding relationship had become both deep and fragile at the same time.

I don't remember much about that day, but I do remember a few specific details. I remember texting some close, trusted friends and, of course, my mom (none of whom audibly cringed or said they had reservations about Dan). I also remember taking my lunch break in my car, so that I could pray and talk to God about all of this. And I also listened to music, straining to find some answer in the songs. One word kept coming to my mind over and over again, like a breath, a whisper: "Redemption."

I didn't know what it meant or what it would look like, but I knew that I was being given the opportunity to extend grace to Dan, even if we didn't end up together. Perhaps all I'd gone through was leading to this, preparing me in some way? Peace—the kind that doesn't make sense—flooded me. I knew God was in this, so I chose to walk forward into the unknown with Dan. The next day we went on our second date, and then were married a little over a year later. In a few months, we will have been married for two years, and we're deliriously cute and happy together. Married life with him is bliss (as corny as that sounds)!

Having read this book, and now knowing what I've gone through prior to meeting Dan, you may think I'm naïve. Or maybe that I'm an idiot. That's okay. You're entitled to your opinion. But for me, the pivotal fact in all of this is that my trust doesn't lie in Dan alone. Yes, I've seen both how hard he works for his sobriety and how important recovery is to him. He wouldn't have bravely shared his story with me if this weren't true. In fact, I've never known anyone doing more for their own well-being and mental health than this man of mine. He inspires me *every* single day, and yes, I'm proud of him. Immensely so.

But my trust does not solely rely on Dan. He could relapse at any moment. And the odds are that he will—even numerous times. So rather, my trust must lie with the God who saw fit to take two broken people and bring them together.

Against the odds, God decided to use our damaged pieces to point to the hope that can only be found in him. He is the only one who will never fail me. He's shown me that time and again.

So whether I'm reminding my husband of that in his moments of self-loathing and shame, or reminding myself in moments when his addiction touches my larger pain body (my fear of being lied to or abandoned), the truth remains the same for both of us. We can be restored.

The power of the gospel means I am loved. Even when I'm feeling unloved or unworthy, even when everything hurts, even when I'm scared or don't know how our story may end, even though I know I don't deserve to be, I am still loved. Endlessly. Unfailingly. Christ suffered horribly, bled, and died in my place to give me peace with God, to break down the barrier of shame I build to "protect" myself, to bind the gaping wounds this life has dealt. Jesus heals the deep pain others have caused. He sees through my efforts to appear good in the ways I've caused deep pain to others. He points to my brokenness, ugliness, and feeble attempts to save myself. He says to me, "Let me see that. Show it to me. Let me love the *real* you." He sees beauty in my mess of a life, and still chooses to redeem me. It's because of *this* love that I'm able to love anyone else, including my husband. I know I'm going to fail Dan, and that he will fail too. We're screwed if our foundation is only the flawed love we have for each other. Dan's screwed if his confidence is only my steadfast support of him at all times. I'm screwed if my hope is only in him never relapsing or perfectly loving me forever.

There's a hope in someone greater. Someone whose love never fails. Regardless of what the future holds or how our story together may end, this is our theme. We are loved. We are God's. So I'm *all in*, along for the ride, wherever he wants to take us. We just want all of it to point to him.

God longs for this to be the theme of everyone's story; yes, even *your* story—the one that may feel beyond redemption and without hope. Maybe the present chapter of your life is black as night. Maybe you want to end everything because the pain is so excruciating and you don't feel like you can make it for one more second. Maybe it just doesn't feel worth it anymore. Maybe you feel completely alone, utterly worthless, like an unlovable piece of garbage. I've truly been there. But I want to remind you that this same love I just mentioned exists for you too! Whoever you are, wherever you are, and no matter what you've done or gone through, you are loved by the same God who spun planets into orbit and paints the sunset each night. He created you. He knows you. He loves the sound of your laugh. He catches every tear that falls from your eyes. He is closer to you than your own breath. He's with you at night, in the dark, when you can't sleep and your mind won't stop reliving your mistakes or the way(s) you've been hurt. He wants to heal you. He gave everything so that you would know how loved you are. He experienced complete separation from God so that you would *never* have to. There is hope for you. There is hope for your story. I pray that all those reading these words will encounter God's unfailing love, and that you'll allow your story to be redeemed by it.

Appendix A: Resources

Books

Bird, Chad. *Night Driving: Notes from a Prodigal Soul.* Grand Rapids: Eerdmans, 2017.

Brand, Russell. *Recovery: Freedom From Our Addictions.* New York: Holt, 2017.

Beattie, Melody. *The New Codependency: Help and Guidance for Today's Generation.* New York: Simon & Schuster, 2010.

Black, Claudia, and Cara Tripodi. *Intimate Treason: Healing the Trauma for Partners Confronting Sex Addiction.* Las Vegas: Central Recovery, 2012.

Carnes, Patrick. *Don't Call It Love: Recovery from Sexual Addiction.* New York: Bantam, 1991.

Channing, Maureen. *Lust, Anger, and Love: Understanding Sexual Addiction and the Road to Healthy Intimacy.* Naperville, IL: Sourcebooks, 2008.

Dines, Gail. *Pornland: How Porn Has Hijacked Our Sexuality.* Boston: Beacon, 2012.

Fradd, Matt. *The Porn Myth: Exposing the Reality Behind the Fantasy of Pornography.* San Francisco: Ignatius, 2017.

Harris, Joshua. *Sex Is Not the Problem (Lust Is): Sexual Purity in a Lust-Saturated World.* Colorado Springs: Multnomah, 2005.

Jenson, Kristen A., Gail A. Poyner, and Debbie Fox. *Good Pictures Bad Pictures: Porn-Proofing Today's Young Kids.* Richland, WA: Glen Cove, 2017.

Maltz, Wendy, and Larry Maltz. *The Porn Trap: A Guide to Healing from Porn Addiction, for Sufferers and Their Loved Ones.* New York: Collins, 2009.

Paul, Pamela. *Pornified: How Pornography Is Damaging Our Lives, Our Relationships, and Our Families.* New York: Holt, 2006.

Steffens, Barbara A., and Marsha Means. *Your Sexually Addicted Spouse: How Partners Can Cope and Heal.* Far Hills, NJ: New Horizon, 2010.

Szalavitz, Maia. *Unbroken Brain: A Revolutionary New Way of Understanding Addiction.* New York: Picador St. Martin's, 2017.

Tiede, Vicki. *When Your Husband Is Addicted to Pornography: Healing Your Wounded Heart.* Greensboro, NC: New Growth, 2012.

Weiss, Douglas. *Partners: Healing from His Addiction.* Colorado Springs: Discovery, 2001.

Weiss, Robert. *Sex Addiction 101: A Basic Guide to Healing from Sex, Porn, and Love Addiction.* Deerfield Beach, FL: Health Communications, 2015.

Workbooks

Carnes, Patrick. *Facing the Shadow: Starting Sexual and Relationship Recovery: A Gentle Path to Beginning Recovery from Sex Addiction.* Carefree, AZ: Gentle Path, 2015.

Cashwell, Craig S., Pennie K. Johnson, and Patrick Carnes. *Shadows of the Cross: A Christian Companion to Facing the Shadow.* Carefree, AZ: Gentle Path, 2015.

Online

Anti-Pornography. http://www.antipornography.org.
Beggar's Daughter. http://www.beggarsdaughter.com.
Celebrate Recovery. http://www.celebraterecovery.com.
Co-Dependents Anonymous International. http://www.coda.org.
Covenant Eyes. http://www.covenanteyes.com.
Dirty Girls Ministries. http://www.dirtygirlsministries.com.
Educate and Empower Kids. http://www.educateempowerkids.org.
Fight the New Drug. http://www.fightthenewdrug.org.
Integrity Restored. http://www.integrityrestored.com.
National Center on Sexual Exploitation. http://www.endsexualexploitation.org.
NoFap. http://www.nofap.org.
Pink Cross Foundation. http://www.thepinkcross.org.
Porn Proof Kids (blog). http://www.pornproofkids.com.
PornHelp. http://www.pornhelp.org.
Protect Young Minds. http://www.protectyoungminds.org.
Pure Desire Ministries. http://www.puredesire.org.
Reboot Nation. http://www.rebootnation.org.
S-Anon International Family Groups. http://www.sanon.org.
Sex Addicts Anonymous. http://www.saa-recovery.org.
Sex and Love Addicts Anonymous. http://www.slaafws.org.
Sexaholics Anonymous. http://www.sa.org.
Sexual Compulsives Anonymous. http://www.sca-recovery.org.
Teen Safe. http://www.teensafe.com.
The Togetherness Project. http://www.togethernessproject.org.
Wired for Intimacy http://www.wiredforintimacy.blogspot.com.
XXX Church. http://www.xxxchurch.com.
Your Brain on Porn. http://www.yourbrainonporn.com.

Appendix B: Prayers

The Jesus Prayer

Lord Jesus Christ, Son of God, have mercy on me, a sinner.

The Serenity Prayer

God, grant me the serenity to accept the things I cannot change, the courage to change the things I can, and the wisdom to know the difference. Living one day at a time, enjoying one moment at a time; accepting hardship as a pathway to peace; taking as Jesus did, this sinful world as it is, not as I would have it; trusting that you will make all things right if I surrender to your will; so that I may be reasonably happy in this life and supremely happy with you forever in the next. Amen.

The Third Step Prayer

God, I offer myself to thee—to build with me and do with me as thou wilt. Relieve me of the bondage of self, that I may better do thy will. Take away my difficulties, that victory over them may bear witness to those I would help of thy power, thy love, and thy way of life. May I do thy will always.

The Prayer of St. Francis of Assisi (Eleventh Step Prayer)

Lord, make me an instrument of thy peace. That where there is hatred, I may bring love. That where there is wrong, I may bring the spirit of forgiveness. That where there is discord, I may bring harmony. That where there is error, I may bring truth. That where there is doubt, I may bring faith. That where there is despair, I may bring hope. That where there are shadows, I may bring light. That where there is sadness, I may bring joy. Lord, grant that I may seek rather to comfort, than to be comforted. To understand, than to be understood. To love, than to be loved. For it is by self-forgetting that one finds. It is by forgiving that one is forgiven.

The Prayer of Release

Heavenly Father, I release to you the burdens that I have been carrying, burdens that you never intended for me to carry. I cast all my cares upon you—all my worries, all my fears. You have told me to not be anxious about anything, but rather to bring everything to you in prayer with thankfulness.

Father, calm my restless spirit, quiet my anxious heart, still my troubling thoughts with the assurance that you are in control. I let go of my grip upon the things I have been hanging onto, with opened hands I come to you. I release to your will all that I am trying to manipulate; I release to your authority all that I am trying to control; I release to your timing all that I have been striving to make happen.

I thank you for your promise to sustain me, preserve me, and guard all that I have entrusted to your keeping. Protect my heart and mind with your peace, the peace that passes all understanding. Father, may your will be done in my life, in your time, and in your way.

The Believing Prayer

Lord, I realize that it is my fault that I am in this predicament. I come to your throne looking for mercy. My request is not based on any merit of my own, but upon your great heart. I believe what the Bible says about you. You are a God of mercy and compassion, and I believe that you will help me out of this mess because of what you are like.

The Prayer of Gratitude

Holy Father, I have amends to make to you, to those in my life, and to myself. In this moment, though, I offer my heart to you with thanks that I can lay down the lies and deceit that have been such a large part of my life for so long. Now I stand, not in the darkness of my lies, deceit, and addiction(s), but in the shadow of the cross. Amid the difficulties that I know lie ahead, help me to always know you are with me. I love you and thank you for loving me just as I am in this moment.

Bibliography

American Psychiatric Association. *Diagnostic and Statistical Manual of Mental Disorders: DSM-5*. Arlington, VA: American Psychiatric Association, 2013.

Barna Group and Josh McDowell Ministry. *The Porn Phenomenon: The Impact of Pornography in the Digital Age*. Ventura, CA: Barna Group, 2016.

Beattie, Melody. *Codependent No More: How to Stop Controlling Others and Start Caring for Yourself*. Center City, MN: Hazelden, 2016.

Carnes, Patrick. *Out of the Shadows: Understanding Sexual Addiction*. Center City, MN: Hazelden, 2001.

Celebrate Recovery. http://www.celebraterecovery.com.

Cloud, Henry, and John Sims Townsend. *Boundaries: When to Say Yes, How to Say No to Take Control of Your Life*. Grand Rapids: Zondervan, 2017.

Co-Dependents Anonymous International. http://coda.org/.

Crichton, Michael. *The Great Train Robbery*. New York: Harper, 2008.

DeSilva, David. *Honor, Patronage, Kinship & Purity: Unlocking New Testament Culture*. Downers Grove, InterVarsity, 200.

Doidge, Norman. *The Brain That Changes Itself: Stories of Personal Triumph from the Frontiers of Brain Science*. New York: Viking, 2007.

Elwell, Walter, and Barry J. Beitzel, editors. *Baker Encyclopedia of the Bible*. Grand Rapids: Baker, 1997.

Fight the New Drug (organization). *Fortify: The Fighter's Guide to Overcoming Pornography Addiction*. Sanger, CA: Familius, 2015.

———. "How Porn Kills Love." May 4, 2017. https://fightthenewdrug.org/how-porn-kills-love/.

Johnson, Eric. *Foundations for Soul Care: A Christian Psychology Proposal*. Downers Grove, IL: InterVarsity, 2007.

Karen, Robert. "Shame." *Atlantic Monthly*, February 1992, 40–70.

Kittel, Gerhard, Geoffrey W. Bromiley, and Gerhard Friedrich, editors. *Theological Dictionary of the New Testament*. Grand Rapids: Eerdmans, 2006.

Kühn, Simone, and Jürgen Gallinat. "Brain Structure and Functional Connectivity Associated with Pornography Consumption: The Brain on Porn." *JAMA Psychiatry* 71 (2014) 827–34.

Lamont, Tom. "Life After the Ashley Madison Affair." *The* Guardian, February 28, 2016. https://www.theguardian.com/technology/2016/feb/28/what-happened-after-ashley-madison-was-hacked.

Lewis, C. S. *The Lion, the Witch and the Wardrobe.* New York: Macmillan, 1950.

———. *Mere Christianity.* San Francisco: Harper, 2001.

"List of Countries by Projected GDP." *Statistics Times*, May 6, 2018. http://www.statisticstimes.com/economy/countries-by-projected-gdp.php.

Maslow, Abraham. "A Theory of Human Motivation." *Psychological Review* 50/4 (1943) 370–96.

National Safety Council. "NSC Motor Vehicle Fatality Estimates." 2018. https://www.nsc.org/portals/0/documents/newsdocuments/2018/december_2017.pdf.

Sprinkle, Preston. *People to Be Loved: Why Homosexuality Is Not Just an Issue.* Grand Rapids,: Zondervan, 2015.

Struthers, William M. *Wired for Intimacy: How Pornography Hijacks the Male Brain.* Downers Grove, IL: InterVarsity, 2009.

Substance Abuse and Mental Health Services Administration (SAMSA). *Results from the 2016 National Survey on Drug Use and Health: Detailed Tables.* September 7, 2017. https://www.samhsa.gov/data/sites/default/files/NSDUH-DetTabs-2016/NSDUH-DetTabs-2016.pdf.

Svendsen, Joseph. *Fundamentalist: Stories of a Mentally Ill, Obsessive Compulsive, Legalistic Youth Group Kid Turned Pastor.* Seattle: BC Words, 2016.

Taylor, Seth, and David Glenn Taylor. *Feels Like Redemption: The Pilgrimage to Health and Healing.* Los Angeles: Fireproof Ministries, 2014.

"Test Yourself." Sexaholics Anonymous. https://www.sa.org/test/.

Tullian, Tchividjian. *Jesus + Nothing = Everything.* Wheaton, IL: Crossway, 2011.

Toates, Frederick. *How Sexual Desire Works: The Enigmatic Urge.* Cambridge: Cambridge University Press, 2014.

Weinschenk, Susan. "100 Things You Should Know about People: #8 – Dopamine Makes You Addicted to Seeking Information." *The Team W Blog*, November 7, 2009. http://www.blog.theteamw.com/2009/11/07/100-things-you-should-know-about-people-8-dopamine-makes-us-addicted-to-seeking-information/.

Wilson, Gary. *Your Brain on Porn: Internet Pornography and the Emerging Science of Addiction.* Kent, UK: Commonwealth, 2014.

Worth Health Organization. *International Statistical Classification of Diseases and Related Health Problems.* Geneva: World Health Organization, 2016.

Your Brain on Porn. https://www.yourbrainonporn.com/.

62854113R00067

Made in the USA
Columbia, SC
05 July 2019